PRAISE F
Entry-Level Life

"In every generation idealism must bite the dust. But it rarely does so with as much good humor as in Mr. Zevin's new book."
—*The New York Times*

"Hilarious." —*The Miami Herald*

"A hysterical, insightful parody." —*The Boston Globe*

"The perfect graduation gift . . . A handbook for those not quite ready to turn in their knapsacks for a briefcase."
—*USA Today*

"A very funny book . . . If you feel like you're masquerading in the real world, Zevin is talking to you."
—Los Angeles *Daily News*

PRAISE FOR
The Nearly-wed Handbook

"Grade: A." —*Entertainment Weekly*

"Comic relief . . . A tome of nerves and neurosis." —*Elle*

"Hilarious and stress-relieving." —*CNN.com*

Also by Dan Zevin

*Entry-Level Life: A Complete Guide to
Masquerading as a Member of the Real World*

*The Nearly-wed Handbook: How to Survive the
Happiest Day of Your Life*

The Day I Turned

Uncool

• • •

The Day I Turned
Uncool

• • •

Confessions of a Reluctant Grown-up

Dan Zevin

Villard Ⓥ New York

This is a work of nonfiction. However, the author has changed some names and other identifying characteristics because it seemed like the adult thing to do.

All rights reserved under International and Pan-American Copyright Conventions. Published in the United States by Villard Books, a division of Random House, Inc., New York, and simultaneously in Canada by Random House of Canada Limited, Toronto.

VILLARD and "V" CIRCLED DESIGN are registered trademarks of Random House, Inc.

Some material originally appeared in a slightly different form in *The Boston Phoenix*.

Library of Congress Cataloging-in-Publication Data is available.

ISBN: 0-8129-6722-4

Villard Books website address: www.villard.com

Printed in the United States of America

9 8 7 6 5 4 3

Book design by Ralph Fowler

For my father, The Ronald.

Acknowledgments

The author would like to express his gratitude to Stephanie Booth, Leslie Brokaw, Tyler Clements, Bruce Gellerman, Karen Gerwin, Steve Heuser, Lily King, Nicole Lamy, Brian McLendon, Steve Messina, Maryanne O'Hara, Dan Rembert, Audrey Schulman, Megan Tingley, Bruce Tracy, Jennifer Rudolph Walsh, Ted Weesner Jr., Katie Zug, and the zoo-crew morning team at the Someday Café.

Contents

Contents

Introduction

We were dumpster-diving, résumé-embellishing peons creeping our ways up the ladder and crashing in apartments with more roommates than rooms. In retrospect, we were having a blast. We went out on weeknights, and did not become hung over after drinking two beers. We subsisted on happy-hour pizza rolls, blissfully unaware that a sensible approach to nutrition entails a 40-30-30 ratio of carbs to protein to fat (unsaturated). When we heard the phrase "open house," we did not envision the chance to inspect a split-level with an open floor plan. We envisioned the chance to attend a Dionysian blowout where the entire world was welcome, at least until the cops shut it down when the old guy next door complained about the futons flying out the window.

And then, out of nowhere, came the day we developed a disturbing new interest in lawn care. The day we ordered Pinot Grigio instead of Pabst. The day we refused to see any concert where we could not sit down (and even then, only after a little nap). I speak, of course, of the day we turned uncool.

For me, it happened over the course of many, many days. I was never exactly Fonz-like to begin with, but now I find myself leading a life I used to think only *old* people led.

Confession: I played golf. Confession: I hired a cleaning lady. Confession: I am the owner of the Turbo nose-hair trimmer with optional ear-hair accessory.

Can I tell you something? Last Saturday night I elected to stay home instead of going to this restaurant downtown because I got a little panicky about the parking situation. The most intense drug experience I've had in recent memory involved double-dosing on ibuprofen, which, incidentally, you've got to try if you—like me—have been jonesing for a mind-blowing anti-inflammatory. Not too long ago, if you asked me to hook you up with free tickets, or a fake ID, or a cheap summer sublet, I'd give you ten people to call off the top of my head. Now I find myself recommending extermi-nators. Need a *roofer*? You have come to the right guy. I've also got an accountant, a therapist, a mechanic, a lawyer, a stockbroker, a house painter (exterior), a house painter (interior); numerous medical personnel, including a first-rate dental hygienist; a tailor, a tiler, a travel agent, an electrician; and some guy who comes over every six months to "snake out" my main plumbing line because tree roots get caught in the pipes.

I do not yet have an assistant, but my wife does (did I mention I also have one of those?), and we do not yet have children, but we do have a dog, which I treat like a child, because I am abnormally in love with her, to the point where sometimes I take her to Petco on a weekend afternoon and let her pick out a special treat—a jumbo bag of pig ears, per-haps—and then later I'll tell my friends all about it, and my friends will pretend to be interested at first, but then they will start slipping into a coma, because they cannot believe that I have turned into the type of individual who goes on and on and on about his friggin' dog.

And to tell you the truth, I can't believe I've turned into that type of individual either. I still think of myself as young, and with-it, which, obviously, I am not. I mean, reread that last sentence. Who says, "with-it"?

I will tell you who. Practicing members of the adult-oriented lifestyle—a crowd I've never felt particularly comfortable with. I suppose I'm what you'd call a reluctant grown-up, living in a perpetual state of astonishment that, yes, it is really me who has strategically placed three (3) fire extinguishers throughout his home, and, yup, it's none other than I who has somehow become one of those responsible neighbors who always buys enough Halloween candy.

Confession: I still relate more to JDs who set off M-80s than to safety-first geeks who collect fire extinguishers.

Confession: I kind of miss trick-or-treating.

A panel of licensed professionals might diagnose me with some kind of Peter Pan complex or arrested-development syndrome that condemns me to the tormented life of a child (or, in my case, a smartass fifteen-year-old) trapped inside a grown man's body. And to them I say: Sounds about right to me.

But I also happen to have my own slant on the situation. I happen to think it is very healthy to be a reluctant grown-up. It sure beats being a *regular* grown-up. Regular grown-ups lead regular lives. They fret about their 401(k)'s and lose sleep over their receding hairlines. They use words like "interface" and "multitask," and they are not even kidding. They commute to regular jobs and wear regular clothes and never, under any circumstances, become "irregular," because they take their fiber consumption extremely seriously. Regular grown-ups call the cops on the kids having a party down the block, and they do not feel even a little guilty, because they do not remember when those kids used to be them. They have more regular things to worry about. The stress of the dishwasher repairman who said he'd come three weeks ago but has now stopped returning their calls. The troubling possibility that their favorite spin-class professor is about to accept a position at another club.

But we reluctant grown-ups, we don't take ourselves all that seriously. We can see the *humor* in the fact that we keep a special flashlight in the glove compartment, just in case of emergencies. We think it is actually kind of *funny* when we discover that one of the many millions of reminders we've written to ourselves actually reads: "Get Woolite." The fact that we recently found ourselves saying, "I used to know you when you were this big" to our friend's younger brother? *It is to laugh.*

The confessions that follow reveal the intimate details of my own ongoing attempts to be a grown-up. I share them not as cautionary tales, but in the hopes that they will inspire you, too, to remain reluctant. Because, my friend, I've got news for you. The day you start feeling like one of those "regular" grown-ups is the day you *really* turn uncool.

The Day I Turned
Uncool

. . .

Hole in None

LIKE MANY reluctant grown-ups, I've always had an aversion to the activity of golf. As a kid, I didn't even get what was so great about miniature golf, at least not until I figured out how to climb into the windmill and set off the hole-in-one bell. But normal golf? To my way of thinking, it was best left to nursing-home patients who didn't have enough stamina for bingo.

Imagine my surprise when some of my own best friends began giving a shit about the U.S. Open. Or worse, when some of my own best friends began turning into golfers themselves. Lately, they've all been peer-pressuring me into participating. "Dan, you gotta try it," they say. "Once you try it, you'll want to do it again and again."

This was the way they used to talk about Xtasy. And let me tell you, they were right about that.

• • •

My day of golf began on the driving range, where I was greeted by my instructor, Ben, a toothsome, Casual Friday kind of guy in Dockers, a striped polo shirt, and those two-tone saddle shoes favored by high school cheerleaders. Looking around, I noticed that almost everyone on the range was also wearing the cheerleader shoes, not to mention a spectacular array of devil-may-care trousers. I myself sported jeans and high-tops, but Ben assured me that I wasn't violating any dress codes since I was also wearing a "soft-collar shirt." I assured Ben that, to the best of my knowledge, I do not own any hard-collar shirts.

I liked Ben. He had a pleasant laugh and the patient demeanor of a special ed. teacher. Which was a very good thing, since I was going to be his pupil.

"Okay! First we'll work on our stance," Ben began, handing me a pitching wedge, which I assumed meant you're supposed to swing it like a baseball bat, which was one of many faulty assumptions I made throughout the day. "Now, flex your knees and stick your seat way out." I appreciated Ben's use of the word "seat," but I frankly found this stance to be a bit swish. Without really thinking about it, I assumed a sort of GI Joe stance instead—a chest out, shoulders back kind of look.

"We've really got to work on loosening you up," said Ben.

After giving up on the stance, we moved on to the grip.

Ben explained that the first grip we'd learn was the Varden Overlap Grip, which I found scary because it led me to believe there would be other grips. And there were. There was the interlock grip, the ten-finger grip, a grip where you're supposed to put your thumb over your index finger, another where you put your index finger over your thumb, and numerous other grips best suited to the double-jointed. I finally settled on the Zevin Death Grip, so-named because it prevented Ben from reconfiguring my fingers into any further grips.

At some point I asked Ben if we might whack a few balls before nightfall. He cheerfully obliged, demonstrating proper alignment by sticking out his seat, taking a swing, and sending his ball soaring into the solar system. Now *that* was pretty awesome, I thought.

Then it was my turn. He handed me a seven-iron, but he may as well have handed me a weed-whacker, since the only thing I sent soaring was a large clump of driving range. This was identified as a "divot shot" by Ben, and it turned out to be my major strength. Far be it from me to boast, but my hand-eye coordination was so consistent that I doubt the driving range has been the same since I left.

Unless they've resodded.

• • •

"Okay! I want you to really concentrate on loosening up." Ben reiterated this advice as I drove our golf cart around the nine-hole course where we spent the rest of the day. By this point, I had finally found something I liked about golf: the cart.

I liked the cart on a couple of levels: (a) it brought back fond memories of doing doughnuts on the manicured yard of Mrs. Schline, who made the mistake of calling the cops that time I had a party in tenth grade, and (b) it was an energy-efficient way to search for the three or four balls I managed not to divot. These balls generally wound up in "the bunkers," defined as those areas of the course you are supposed to aim *away* from, such as sand traps, marshes, and craniums of fellow golfers.

The bunker I became most intimate with was the sand trap, though I have been wondering what happened to the gentleman with the salmon trousers who disappeared somewhere around the third hole.

We were well ahead of schedule upon arriving at the ninth hole, mainly because I drove us straight past holes four through eight. The way I saw it, if I wanted to spend the day in the sand, I would have gone to the beach. The final hole was a par five, meaning it was supposed to take five shots to get it in. I was around my eleventh when I saw something I liked even more than the golf cart. It was called the Beverage Cart. You heard me correctly.

The beverage-cart lady asked what I wanted, and I ordered a stiff Bloody Mary, the golfiest drink I could think of. As for Ben, he was a blue Gatorade man. And as I kicked off my shoes, poured out the sand, and sucked down my Bloody, I finally understood what he'd been talking about all day.

To enjoy a game of golf, you just have to loosen up.

Confession:

"I spend a great deal of time engaged in
home-improvement projects."

Repair-Impaired

A T FIRST, building a shelf for the closet
seemed like a good idea. And it would've
been, if I were one of those hands-on, do-
it-yourself guys for whom home repair is second nature. Unfortunately, I'm one of those hands-off, do-it-someone-else
guys for whom home repair is a humiliating descent into the
depths of incompetence. For I am repair-impaired.

Do you want to know the contents of my toolbox? Here
is the list: thumbtacks. Okay, I lied. I don't even have a toolbox. I have a shoe box. A shoe box filled with glue. Not just
Elmer's, either. I have waterproof silicone glue, three kinds
of contact cement, Liquid Nails Heavy-Duty Construction
and Remodeling Adhesive. Like all of us for whom a "shop"

is strictly a place to buy—as opposed to *sand*—things, I have used glue as a crutch. Things I have recently glued include:

- coat rack (to wall)
- refrigerator vent (to refrigerator)
- headlight (to car)

And if you think I'm being facetious about that last one, it is obvious that you've never worked with a dual-tube mixing pac of two-ton epoxy.

I have no doubt that I inherited my disability from my father, the same man I hold responsible for my nose. My father is a doctor. He knows how to deliver a baby. He does not know how to hammer. When I was little, I'd sit at the dinner table, enthralled by his tales of life-saving surgery. But every now and then, something would disrupt his train of thought.

Dad: Today I did a quadruple oophorectomy and— *UH-OH! Light is no longer coming out of that glass thing on the ceiling!*

Me: I guess the bulb blew out.

Dad: I'll call Bob Duris.

Bob Duris was this all-purpose Mr. Fix-It character we nonhandymen look upon with a mix of awe and envy. He possessed tools that required extension cords. When he hammered, he stored the nails in his *teeth*. Bob Duris could assess any home improvement task by instinct. "Yep, Doc, looks like your garage-door opener needs a new battery," Bob Duris would say.

I've established a vast network of pro bono Bobs over the years: roommates; landlords; the owner of Masse Hardware, whom I once lured to my leaky toilet with the bribe of a bottle of gin. When the good-natured ribbing began ("Q: How many Zevins does it take to screw in a lightbulb? A: A *what*?") I just played along. But last year, everything changed. Last year, my wife, Megan, and I moved into our "starter home" in North Cambridge, a modest abode located on the wrong side of the Harvard Square tracks.

If you are a realtor, you would refer to this house as a fixer-upper. If you are an honest person, however, you would call it a shithole. Before I knew it, Megan was drilling, spackling, cutting out pages from *The Modern Woman's Guide to Home Repair*. I began sneak-reading this tome one night when she was off at Home Depot. She returned to find me soaking wet, shouting expletives at the drainpipe.

"Oh, you don't have to worry about that," she said. "I already asked Jeffrey and Rick to help me with that."

Jeffrey and Rick, it should be noted, are *my* friends. It was one thing for *me* to call them whenever I was too incompetent to fix something myself. But it was another thing for *her* to call them whenever I was too incompetent to fix something myself. Suddenly, I felt like a big Nancy-boy in front of my wife. I had to do something to reclaim my manhood. I had to put a shelf in the closet.

And so it is in hopes that I may be an inspiration to the repair-impaired throughout the land that I now leave you with . . .

The Reluctant Grown-up's Guide to Basic Closet Shelf Installation (Share It with Someone You Love)

STEP 1: *Estimate Time Required for Home-Improvement Task*

Based on my experience, a good rule of thumb is: 5 minutes estimated time = 5 years actual time.

STEP 2: *Obtain a Shelf*

As a budding handyman, I determined that I needed a really big shelf because this was a really big closet. Using my Lucite "Virginia Is For Lovers" ruler, I measured the area (ten by about eleven rulers) and proceeded to Home Depot to secure a piece of wood. It is not advised to arrive at Home Depot the day they decide they'll no longer cut wood to size.

STEP 3: *Cut Wood to Size*

To do this, I found it necessary to buy a saw (sharp cutting implement available wherever you buy glue). Actually, I found it necessary to buy many saws—a jigsaw, a hacksaw, a circular saw, a rhombus saw—each of which proved to be a more inappropriate saw for the job than the saw that preceded it. What I learned from this experience is: it is best not to over-saw. You'll know it's time to stop when your wood begins to warp due to the amount of perspiration that is pouring off your forehead.

STEP 4: *Attempt to Insert Shelf in Closet*

At long last, I was ready to reap the rewards of my foray into home improvement. I hoisted the shelf into the closet, balanced it atop the clothes-hanger rod, and stepped back to gaze upon my achievement. It was then that I realized I had done something more here than just build a shelf. I had built a shelf with no support brackets. And as it came crashing down, producing a fresh new gash in the floor, a strange calm came over me. I am not a failure, just a beginner, I realized. My wife does not think I am a Nancy-boy just because I cannot install a shelf in the closet. I excel at other things, such as gluing.

All of this brings me to the last but most important step for the nonhandyman who is considering engaging in home improvement activities.

STEP 5: *Call Bob Duris*

Confession:

"I am a figure of authority."

Back to School

O N MY FIRST day of school, the kid sitting next to me raised his hand and made the following inquiry: "Professor, does that count toward our final grade?" I, for one, was taken aback, not so much by the question, but by the odd understanding that it was being asked to *me*. He may as well have called me Your Honor, or Captain, or some other title best reserved for serious, responsible figures of authority. "Professor"? That would suggest I had something to profess.

In reality, the job was called Part-Time Faculty Adjunct Instructor, a title best reserved for freelancers so starved for human contact, they will do anything for a chance to get out of the house. I got it through my friend Ted, a fellow man of letters who supports his habit by pinch-teaching at local colleges. The class was to cover magazine journalism, a field I did know a little something about, having written many a magazine article, including but not limited to "How to Fake a Résumé" and "A Guide to the Guts: Where to Find the Easiest Courses on Your Campus," neither of which I elected to share with the dean who interviewed me for the job. Now was not the time to present myself as a sophomoric weisenheimer. Now was the time to present myself as a serious, responsible figure of authority. Now was the time to present myself as one of Them.

I arrived forty-five minutes early for that first class, since being one of Them was a role requiring ample time for adjustment. I'd spent most of the morning adjusting my wardrobe. What does a serious, responsible figure of authority wear, I wondered. Elbow patches? Wallabies? Would I be sending the wrong message if I showed up in jeans? ("Look! I am just like one of you, so you don't have to listen to a word I say!") or would jeans work to my advantage? ("Look! I am one of those right-on young teachers who might go drinking with you after class, so you'll want to hang on my every word!") I settled on khakis, a white shirt, and a sweater vest. Where this sweater vest came from I cannot recall, but it was a dark-blue sweater vest, and I remembered reading somewhere that dark blue is the color of authority. Also, I wore a belt. The belt is probably my only fashion accessory that sees less action than the sweater vest.

I began by rearranging all the little desks into assorted configurations: rows, a semicircle, a semi-semicircle, and finally, a full-on, regulation-sized circle. Nowhere in the room did I find a regulation-sized teacher's desk, but I did detect a wooden lectern in front of the blackboard, which was really a whiteboard—one of those plastic-coated deals you need special Magic Markers to write on. The discovery that there were no Magic Markers came as kind of a relief, since it meant I couldn't write on the whiteboard, which would have required standing up and professing, perhaps even pacing over to my lectern every so often where I'd feel even more like some dipshit impostor. I shoved the lectern into the corner, squeezed into a little desk, and flipped through the stack of magazines I brought to show my students . . . what, exactly? That I happened to raid my recycling bin this morning?

It was then, approximately sixteen minutes before class was to begin, that a nun walked in the room.

"Is this the magazine class?" she asked, confirming that she did not somehow confuse Emerson College with Our Lady of Immaculate Conception.

"Sure is!" I answered, overly unfazed that my first-ever student happened to be wearing a habit. Maybe it was one of those college fashion fads inspired by work uniforms, like bike messenger bags, or operating-room shirts. Nun *chic*. Whatever it was, the hat made it hard to tell how old she was, but when I told her she was in the right place, here is what she said: "Cool." This led me to believe she was a young nun; a "nontraditional" student, as they are known. It occurred to me that she was probably wondering what *I* was doing there, a question I was frankly grappling with myself.

"I'm Dan. I'm the, um, teacher." What could I possibly teach a nun? The woman is married to God.

"Cool," she replied. "I'm Sister Madonna."

Soon the rest of the students filed in, a phalanx of Urban Outfitted undergrads with all manner of facial piercings, no manner of nun uniforms. They seemed to know Sister Madonna, and since they didn't look the type to have met in Bible Study Club, I figured they'd had classes with her before. I actually got the feeling it was considered hip to know the nun. "Whaddup, Sister Madonna," I actually heard one of them say.

Don't ask how I ever thought up the innovative ice-breaking exercise of going around the room and talking about our favorite magazines, but that is how I opted to start class. I felt compelled to comment on each magazine that came up, demonstrating my expansive breadth of knowledge for anyone who might have wondered if I was some dipshit impostor. I chose my comments carefully, particularly if I had never heard of the magazines that came up.

"Oh, yes, I too am a charter subscriber to *Glass Eaters,*" I would comment carefully. "But why don't YOU describe its subject matter, just in case anyone in the room has never heard of it."

Over the next few weeks, I'd sometimes surprise myself by blathering on about things I *did* know—discourses called "lectures" by real teachers—but the result was that I'd end up feeling even less like a real teacher. Midway through one of my little talks—that's what I called them, "talks"—I'd glance out into the circle and notice that everybody was staring at me. I guess that goes along with the territory—you talk, they watch—but I found it disruptive. Did I just say something they knew to be patently incorrect? Had they ever experienced this level of boredom in their entire lives?

Their expressions ranged from anesthetized to perplexed to openly hostile. The only student who seemed vaguely interested was this goateed guy named Jeff. Sometimes when I would say something, I noticed Jeff would write it down. I found myself focusing on Jeff, conducting a one-on-one private tutorial for him.

At some point, I extended my field of vision to include not only Jeff, but also Sister Madonna. I mean, she seemed nice enough. The only problem was that she kept doing this thing where she'd scratch her head through her hat, which would make the hat move from side to side, and this of course would cause me to lose my train of thought. So I resumed teaching just Jeff, and he continued writing stuff down, and I felt myself loosening up until it dawned on me that what he was *really* writing down, probably nine hundred million times by now, was this: "Those who can, do; those who can't, teach."

• • •

Some might attribute such anxieties to sheer inexperience. I, however, have arrived at a different theory to explain my unease around the students: I remembered what I was like when I was in their shoes. The joy of getting baked out of my mind before Introduction to Astronomy each morning! The cutting of Western Civ in favor of an enjoyable afternoon handjob! Those perfect spiral notebooks filled nine hundred million times with, "Those who can, do; those who can't, teach."

My biggest problem as a teacher, in other words, was that I could relate to my students. There I'd be, listening attentively as they workshopped their articles, when I'd suddenly become preoccupied by the possibility that any of them—with one fairly obvious exception—could have been copulating ten minutes before coming to class.

It's no wonder that they started treating me more like a peer than a pedagogue—despite my ever-growing selection of sweater vests. Once, I asked if there were any questions about my talk on copyediting. This guy who barely spoke all semester (baked out of his mind, no doubt) raised his hand and asked, "Where do you get your hair cut?" After analyzing the elements of a travel article, another pupil asked if I knew where she could adopt a cat. This prompted perhaps the liveliest class discussion we ever had, not counting the one that started when this girl in a belly shirt asked what my wife looked like. To prevent similar outbursts, I split the class into small workshopping groups. As I circulated around to each group, my presence was met by the following feedback from the same guy who wanted to know where I got my hair cut: "Bro', do you have to hover over us like that? You're makin' me nervous."

It wasn't until midsemester that I employed a teaching technique that enabled my students—not to mention myself—to feel like someone qualified was running the operation. The technique was "guest speakers." Basically, I cold-called anyone in the city with a magazine job and conned them into coming to class. "Your publication embodies everything I've been stressing all semester," I'd tell them on the phone. "It would be such an honor for the students to meet someone so accomplished." If they fell for it, I would run out and buy a copy of their publication, which, nine times out of ten, I had never so much as skimmed.

Farming out my job to those who believed they knew what they were talking about worked beautifully until my all-time favorite art director, a man whose art direction I knew nothing about, came in for his turn at Teacher for a Day. He covered the basics—photojournalism, fonts, you get the picture—when someone asked which magazine designs he most admired. (Lucky for him, she already knew where to adopt a cat.)

"I'm glad you asked that question," he remarked, reaching into his briefcase for a magazine called *Tempo*. The cover of *Tempo* depicted a waist-to-kneecaps portrait of a black gentleman who appeared to be exceptionally aroused.

Please don't talk about *Tempo*, I thought, nervously watching Sister Madonna's reaction from the corner of my eye. She was scratching her hat.

"Well, I'd have to say that *Tempo* is a great example of the risks the Europeans are taking . . ."

Okay, just don't hold it up for her to see.

"Why don't I hold it up so everyone can see . . ."

All right, but whatever you do, do not pass it around.

"How about if we pass it . . ."

Whether or not Sister Madonna got a chance to examine *Tempo*, I do not know. I do know that I spent the rest of the semester trying to redeem myself, hoping to put the Johnson ordeal behind us by turning her into teacher's pet. No matter what she did, she got an A. At one point, the assignment was to work with a partner to create a new magazine.

She ended up working with Jeff. Jeff wanted to do a magazine about underground nightlife. Sister Madonna wanted to do a magazine about religion. I am not proud to report that I said it was a *great* idea to cover clubbing *and* Christianity in one easy-to-read resource. They got an A+.

A lot of it was that I was just afraid of getting in trouble, another post-traumatic symptom easily traced to my erstwhile days as a student. But now that I was the teacher, the risk actually seemed greater. There were these things called Course Evaluation Forms, see, which the students filled out to rate their teachers. I could only imagine Sister Madonna's.

Please use the space below to jot down some general impressions of your instructor:

He is the evil Antichrist whose classroom is a den of sin and filth. He shall be denied salvation to burn in the bowels of hell.

I decided to bag the guest speaker technique, partly because of the Johnson incident but mostly because I ran out of guests. Besides, it had been something like two months by now, and I had come to understand that anesthetized-perplexed-openly-hostile is just the natural facial expression for college students, sort of how "startled" is the natural facial expression for squirrels. Once I stopped taking it personally, I gradually got less inhibited. Not only did I rise from my little desk to write on the whiteboard here and there—sometimes without worrying about my penmanship—but I even screwed up the courage to do the teacheriest thing of all: call on students who were not engaging in "class participation."

For my test case, I called on Jimmy, a particularly hostile-looking sophomore with spiky blue hair. Jimmy's primary method of class participation was clicking his tongue stud between his teeth.

"So what did everyone think of Tom Wolfe's article on new journalism? Jimmy, how about you?"

"Uh," Jimmy replied, "it reminded me of that thing you suggested the other day about putting yourself into the story instead of being an anonymous reporter. I'm trying to do that with my own articles now."

Here was my initial reaction: *Did I say something about putting yourself into the story instead of being an anonymous reporter?* But then I thought: Why, yes, I did! I *DID* say something about putting yourself into the story instead of being an anonymous reporter. I don't *remember* saying something about putting yourself into the story instead of being an anonymous reporter, but obviously, I said it, because scary Jimmy here was so influenced, so *profoundly moved* by whatever I said, that he is trying to do this thing with his *own* articles now!

I am at a loss to convey how exhilarating this was, this notion that I had inadvertently taught something to one of my students. Indeed, it gave me the confidence to pursue my calling as an educator, and I've since part-time-faculty-instructed a total of four other classes. No more do I disguise myself in sweater vests, or worry about the whiteboard. As a matter of fact, I recently purchased my own personal set of multicolored DryErase Markers (chisel tipped).

Whenever I feel like it, I let my students leave early, because I am the one in charge, you understand. And rarely if ever do I censor my speech, avoiding phrases like "for Christ's sake" just in case there might be a nun in the room. Yes, I have learned much about the teaching game, but the main thing I have learned is that Course Evaluation Forms are not to be feared, but are instead to be distributed on the last day of class with a complimentary selection of Dunkin' Munchkins.

"Yo, Dan the Man!" one of my youngsters greeted me the other day as he walked into class ten minutes late, presumably after a handjob back at the dorm. A few semesters ago, I would have wondered if this was any way to address a serious, responsible figure of authority. But now I don't care. It sure beats "Professor," for Christ's sake.

Fitness Crazed

LAST WEEK, my gym was more crowded than I've ever seen it—no big surprise, considering I've hardly ever seen it. Like many health-club dilettantes, I've been a member on and off for years, a few days after paying membership dues "on," the rest of the year "off." But this year will be different, I tell you, because this year, something has changed: my pants size. I have worn the same pants size since I was a skinny, Stridex-dependent sixteen-year-old in brown Levis corduroys. It has not been easy to face the fact that I am now a person who secretly unbuttons his pants before sitting. At first, I blamed the dryer for shrinking my pants. Then I blamed the dryer for shrinking the waist but not the length of my pants. Finally, I conceded that perhaps it was time to add a cross-training component to my current chew-and-swallow program.

I am pleased to report that I have frequented my gymnasium for two and a half entire weeks in a row, a clear-cut indicator that I will stick with it for the rest of my life. How can *you* become a highly trained model of dedication and discipline such as myself? The first step is to locate the facility where you've been paying membership dues for the past several years. And to help those of you who are as serious as me about sticking with it forever, I have prepared:

The Dan Zevin Workout Guide to Sticking with It Forever

Weights: One thing I have discovered as a dedicated gym-goer is that strength resistance training does not mean you are supposed to *resist* doing strength training. This is unfortunate, since strength training equipment tends to be very heavy. The most useful piece of equipment I have come across is the Walkman. Over the course of my two and a half entire weeks in a row, I've built up to a high-volume routine allowing me to drown out the violent grunting sounds from amateurs who don't realize they wouldn't be grunting if they simply lifted lighter weights. The Walkman also eliminates the stress of piped-in gym Muzak, a bizarre playlist that moves from Julio Iglesias to Chicago to what I can only assume is the Backstreet Boys. But, most important, the Walkman is a deterrent to anyone who asks you for a "spot." A "spot," for readers who do not know because they have not made a lifetime commitment to strength training, is an exercise in which one strength trainer hovers over the other and shouts, "It's all you, baby! Don't stop!" I, for one, believe such language is best reserved for the bedroom. I also believe that standing in front of a mirror while working out is ill-advised. The reason I came to the gym in the first place is because I stood in front of a mirror, and what did I see then? A man with his pants button unbuttoned. I do not need to revisit that disturbing image. I'd much rather hoist R.E.M. into my Walkman and hop aboard a . . .

Stationary Exercise Machine: Making a pledge of pulmonary well-being means not only getting on one of these things but actually *staying* on it, ideally for a duration long enough to figure out how it works. Begin by entering your age, weight, mother's maiden name, gravitational expansion ratio of molecular digitalization, etc. Then begin pedaling, stair-climbing, or getting your shoelace caught in the rotary mechanism and being sucked under the conveyor belt until you are crushed and killed (advanced workout only). When evaluating which device is right for you, I recommend looking only for one that is located in front of a TV. It is also essential to find one with the following features: magazine holder; Walkman holder. The goal is to watch the Sylvester Stallone movie on TV, listen to the R.E.M. tape in your Walkman, and peruse the heart-healthy, tummy-yummy recipes in *Cooking Light* magazine—*all at the same time*. I have found no better cross-training program to keep me happily pedaling in place instead of running to the sauna for a cigarette. And that is because *I* am no longer an armchair athlete. *I* am one of the standout pupils in my . . .

Exercise Class: The class I enrolled in is Abs Class, due to the earlier mentioned pants situation. The good news is that this class does not involve a heavy reading load. The bad news is that it involves in-class assignments like: "Okay, everyone, wrap your legs around your elbows and crunch those obliques!" The other bad news is that it involves class-mates, many of whom tend to perspire. On a related note, I must advise you that the most important prerequisite for Abs Class is that you do not eat a microwaved burrito before class. I once made this mistake and am ashamed to say that it was me who broke wind during Russian Twists last Thurs-day. But did that stop me from matriculating on Friday? No! Because the most important thing of all for a serious student like myself is . . .

Consistency: Once you start going to your gymnasium regularly (two and a half entire weeks in a row, for example), you will begin to notice certain dedicated individuals who are always there. Always. There is a guy at my club whom I have named Robot Man due to the bionic powers he exhibits on a contraption I think is called the Eclipse machine. I have seen Robot Man vigorously eclipsing on a Sunday morning, eight o'clock. I have seen him eclipsing on a Tuesday night at seven-thirty. I happened to drive by my gym on Christmas—one of the only days it is ever closed—and I am certain Robot Man's vehicle was parked outside. There are numer-ous robot men and women at my gymnasium. Sometimes, I find myself thinking, If I really keep it up this time, maybe I, too, will be like them: a relentlessly dedicated exercise android lifting, pedaling, and crunching my life away in front of the mirrored walls of my twenty-four-hour fitness facility.

Maybe I'll just get a bigger pair of pants.

Confession:

"I take pride in my lawn."

· ·

The Grass Is Never Greener

H AVE YOU EVER had that weird feeling when you're in the middle of doing something and you suddenly kind of leave your body, look at yourself in disbelief, and think: Who *is* this person doing this thing? It happened to me most recently while fertilizing. I was jauntily pushing my new drop spreader back and forth over the patch of rubble that would soon be my fertile backyard. When my cell phone rang, I had to remove my special orange gardening mitts before answering.

"So what are you up to today?" asked my friend Mark, unknowingly prompting the reply that would trigger my out-of-body experience.

"*I am just doing some yard work,*" I stated.

Everything was okay once I reentered my body and fin-

27

ished fertilizing. Big deal, so I had a little identity crisis while engaged in yard work. This sort of thing is happening to everyone these days. We suddenly like doing things we once couldn't imagine even thinking about. For some, it's yoga. For others, it's cooking. But for a great many of us, I have noticed, it is yard work. We spend Saturdays combating crabgrass. We secretly fantasize about power mowers. We e-mail each other links to web sites that offer eggplant seeds at wholesale prices.

We first found out about these web sites when our parents e-mailed them to us.

Perhaps you, too, have found yourself drawn to yard work. And perhaps you are wondering: Why yard work, why now? As always, I can only speak for myself.

I. Yard Work Reawakens Your Sense of Discovery

As a first-time property owner, I'll never forget what I thought one day as I gazed proudly upon my patch of land. I thought, Why is it black? On closer inspection, I concluded that it was black because it was blacktop, as opposed to grass, the form of ground cover I guess I'd been expecting. Why the yard was covered in blacktop I did not know. All I knew was that Megan and I missed this detail when we bid on the house because, at the time, most of the blacktop was concealed by snow. And most of the snow was concealed by what looked like some kind of backyard shantytown. The former owners, known around the neighborhood as the Clampetts, landscaped the area with unique features like a car up on cinder blocks, a few giant standing computers, one piano, two tents inhabited by cats, and a colossal pile of rocks that the owner—Jed, we'll call him—referred to as his "mineral collection." It wasn't so much a yard as a junkyard. We always knew we'd have to get rid of the junk. What we didn't know, until the discovery of the blacktop, was that we'd also have to get rid of the yard.

It was unclear to me how one went about this task, no big surprise there. So, I did what I always do in these situations: I consulted an expert. I spotted him in a parking lot when I was walking my dog, Chloe, one morning. I could tell he was an expert because he was wearing a hard hat and operating a jackhammer.

"I'll tell ya who you gotta call for this jawb," he said in a thick Boston accent. "You gotta call Granite Man."

"Excellent, what's his number?"

The guy let loose one of those phlegm-filled laughs that signals an impending coughing seizure.

"Buddy. Granite Man don't call back," he finally said. This was something I'd already come to expect from indoor contractors, so I wasn't exactly shocked that it applied to blacktop removers as well.

"You can find him at Sully's Tap. His truck's always packed outside."

Though Sully's Tap is right around the block, it's the kind of place where guys like me (defined as "guys who do not know how to remove the blacktop from their yard") get the crap beaten out of them. I was a little concerned about showing up uninvited, so I spent a few days stalking the place on my bike. It was true. No matter when I pedaled past, the Granite Man truck was in its usual spot, in front of a fire hydrant. One morning, I noticed a guy staggering out of the bar and into the truck. I could only assume it was Granite Man himself.

I shit you not when I tell you he said, "Who wants to know?" upon being asked his availability. Shortly thereafter, he was in my backyard, having drunk-driven his backhoe over to survey the site. It took him ten minutes to pulverize the place, scooping great chunks of earth right out of the ground, ripping through pavement in a deafening roar, annihilating any and all asphalt in his path. I watched the whole thing from my kitchen window and I've got to say, it was like the coolest thing I've ever seen.

"Two hundred bucks," Granite Man said when he was done.

"I thought we agreed on one-fifty," I answered.

"Whaddaya, Jewish?" he replied.

I gave him $225 and off he went, swerving down the street in his backhoe, headed roughly in the direction of Sully's Tap.

II. Yard Work Is an Exercise in Self-Sufficiency

There's only one thing required to work the land and till the soil. It's called soil. Actually, it's not called soil. It's called "loam," the name given to soil once it stops being dirt and starts being a commodity priced upwards of thirty bucks a yard. Megan and I spent an invigorating five hours one afternoon grading (spreading) this loam (soil), often with the help of our neighbor (Sandy). That's another thing about yard work. It's good for community relations. You'll be amazed at how supportive everyone can be when there is something in it for them, like the sprucing up of a shantytown that has depressed neighborhood property values for years. Unfortunately, yard work can also bring out the worst in certain community members, such as those who might live three doors down from you and might leave you a snippy note one day telling you to rake all the leaves in the middle of the street because they came from *your* tree. I personally do not know any community members like this. And even if I did, I checked the deed to the house, and that tree is not mine.

Another way yard work builds self-sufficiency is that it gives you complete creative control over the type of yard you want. Myself, I've never gone in for that flowery enchanted garden scene with the birdbaths and the lawn gnomes and the weird mirrored balls up on the pedestals. I just wanted a little grass on my loam. Now, according to the color-coded map in *Reader's Digest Lawn Care Basics,* we lived in Zone 1, which immediately ruled out any inclinations we may have had to plant Blue Gamma grass seed, Zoysia grass seed, or Crested Wheatgrass seed. The recommended seed for Zone 1 was Kentucky Bluegrass. I found this rather confusing, since Kentucky itself seemed to be in Zone 2. But who was I to argue? It was news to me that seeds came in any styles beyond, you know, "grass." It was also news to me that you were supposed to spend a day monitoring your yard for sunlight conditions before choosing which *variety* of Kentucky Bluegrass seeds to plant. What follows is a facsimile of my report.

TIME	SUNLIGHT CONDITIONS
7:00 A.M.	shady
9:00 A.M.	shady
11:00 A.M.	pretty fuckin' shady
2:00 P.M.	dark
5:00 P.M.	forgot to look

It was with great gusto that I used my new drop spreader to apply Kentucky Bluegrass Starter Seed, Dense Shade Variety, to my loam. Carefully adhering to the directions in *Reader's Digest,* I made two passes over the property at right angles to each other. I then used the back of my neighbor's rake to gently cover these seeds. I then set forth to fertilize. I then had an out-of-body experience.

I drew the line when the book said to spread hay on the seeds. First of all, where do you get hay? And anyway, it's not like I planned to raise horses or something. I decided the hay was unnecessary. This may have had something to do with the birds. It seemed only seconds after I turned on the sprinkler, a million missile-sized crows came swooping down to feast upon tempting Kentucky Bluegrass seeds, Dense Shade Variety. And I don't know where *you* live, but here in Zone 1, when a swarm of killer crows descends upon your loam, you get the hell out of the way.

III. Yard Work Provides an Emotional Outlet

If you need a break from the hustle-bustle demands of everyday life, yard work will always be there for you. Let me give you an example. Whenever I am faced with a looming work deadline, I'll seize the opportunity to procrastinate with a little mulching. The effect is a lot like doing laundry: it's never what you should *really* be doing, but it makes you feel like a productive and worthwhile human being nonetheless.

There is a rich cornucopia of emotions the reluctant grown-up experiences every day. And if you're like me, you'll find a form of yard work to vent each and every one of them. For instance:

- Do you feel **FRUSTRATED** that the guy you hired to build a deck in your yard, a guy you liked at first because he described his design sense as very "Zen," turned out to be an actual practicing Zen Buddhist who would disappear for several billable hours per day to "meditate," and one afternoon took it upon himself to pour a slab of cement directly on top of the twelve blades of Kentucky Bluegrass you managed to grow earlier in the season, explaining only that he thought it would be a good place to *wipe your feet* before stepping onto the deck?

    If so, I'd recommend doing some **PRUNING.** Using a long-handled lopping shears, envision your Zen deck builder's neck while hacking off those stubborn branches and mumbling some colorful mantras of your own.

- Do you feel **SAD** that the kid you hired to fence in your yard trampled the fifty-seven dollars' worth of pachysandra you planted the previous day, not to mention leaving your loam covered in a thick layer of sawdust? A lengthy dose of obsessive **WEED-ING** is all you need to lift the spirits and regain a sense of order and control.

* Do you feel **ANGRY** because your dog, Chloe, for whom you had the fence installed, has taken to chewing up your deck and defiling your loam? Perhaps it's time to take a break from your private estate and discover some public parks instead. (Please refer to page 68.)

IV. Yard Work Introduces You to a Whole New World

Of all the strange and mysterious places one is drawn to as one gets on in years—the health-food store, the no-smoking section, Crate & Barrel—there is but one that promises to alter the course of one's life. I speak of the garden supply center. For me, it happened at Mahoney's Nursery, an oasis filled with fragrant, flowering shrubs and miles of misty greenhouses. The first time Megan and I went, it was like we'd unlocked the secrets of the natural world. *So this is why that guy on Sherman Street has a pile of rotting garbage by his vegetable patch,* I thought, examining a box of SuperHot Compost Starter and chucking it immediately into my rolling wagon. *Aha! Miracle-Gro Bloom Booster has been specially formulated with a super-high phosphorus content to increase the number of blooms and get more vibrant colors on your rhododendron bushes. Who knew?* Into the wagon it went, along with a rhododendron bush, a No-Clog four-in-one spray nozzle, and a bottle of fox urine—you heard me—that promised to rid my yard of pesky squirrels. At first, it seemed a little strange to purchase fox urine, but considering that I'd already thrown a bag of cow manure in the wagon, I figured, what the heck. Frankly, I would've bought the whole damn fox if they sold them, because when it comes to squirrels, I swear I won't rest until every last one of the suckers has been banished from my loam.

Excuse me a second, I think I feel another one of those out-of-body moments coming on.

Okay, I'm back. Where was I? Oh yeah, the garden supply center. The best part about this place is the expertise of the sales help. They interview you about your drainage situation. They interrogate you about your pH balance. They cross-examine you about your mowing habits.

"Well, right now it's basically still loam," I said to the saleslady who sold me the pee.

"Does the loam have worms in it?" she asked.

"Is it good or bad to have worms?"

"It's good."

"Then I'm sure we don't have any."

"Would you describe the loam as moist and sticky or dry and sandy?"

"Definitely dry and sandy. And cement-y."

"What do you mean, cement-y?"

"I mean there's a chunk of cement in it over by the deck. It's to wipe our feet."

The lady recommended planting moss on the cement, a sensible idea, considering the alternative was calling Granite Man to remove it. Better yet, she hooked me up with this whole new kind of grass seed—Fine Fescues, it's called—that's supposed to be way better for my Zone 1 needs than that

Kentucky Bluegrass shwag *Reader's Digest* recommended. Finally, thanks to her, I've become a proud participant in the Scotts Brand Annual Lawn Care Program, a year-round routine that entails the application of early-spring prolonged-release fertilizer; late-spring post-crabgrass/pre-insect-control fertilization fertilizer; midsummer turf builder with pre-fall, post-spring dandelion and grub control; and, of course, early autumn/late fall winterizer with fungus protection.

Sure it's a lot of work, but it's worth it, because the printed propaganda that came with my Fine Fescues promises "a handsome carpet of thick, luxurious greenery that will be the envy of your neighbors." Just the other day, as a matter of fact, one of my neighbors stopped by as I was blissfully attending to my loam with a beer in one hand and a gardening hose in the other. I can only *hope* his remarks were made in envy, as opposed to something more painful—like honesty.

"Yup, the people who lived here before tried *everything* to get a lawn growing back here," he said. "Finally drove them crazy after a few years and they covered the whole thing up with blacktop."

Confession:

"I am from New Jersey."

No Exit

I
T SEEMS LIKE only yesterday (as does virtually everything that has occurred during my lifetime) that Bruce Springsteen and the E Street Band came through Boston to play the Fleet Center. I wasn't particularly interested at the time. Where I'm from, you just don't shell out a skillion bucks to watch a grown man called "the Boss" prance around a stadium named after a bank. Where I'm from, you shell out a *gajillion* bucks to watch him prance around a stadium named after an airline.

Or sometimes, where I'm from, your father shells out these bucks, because he has decided—inexplicably—that he is taking you, your nineteen-year-old brother, Richie, and your stepmother, Bebe, on a family outing to Continental Airlines Arena to see "the Bruce" (as your father calls him). That is what folks do where *I'm* from.

I'm from new jersey. Wait, let me try that again. I'm from New Jersey! I *AM* from New Jersey. Hello, my name is Dan, and I am from New Jersey. Granted, I presently reside in the Commonwealth of Massachusetts. But after decades of denial, I have finally come to terms with my glorious Garden State heritage.

And I owe it all to the Bruce.

● ● ●

My awakening began unexpectedly, as these things often do. Phone rings, I answer. It's the usual Sunday-night call from my father (a/k/a Ronald Zevin), calling from the house where I grew up in New Jersey. We cover the usual: five-day forecast, cute trick our respective dogs did this week, is my basement dry—but then my old man says something cockamamie. "I know it would be a schlep to come down to Jersey," says Ronald, "but I managed to get tickets to see the Bruce. I thought it would be fun for all of us to go together."

Now, Ronald Zevin is many wonderful things—gifted gynecologist, loyal viewer of *Antiques Roadshow,* dedicated eater of pastrami, to name but a few—but rock 'n' roller is not one of them. The idea that he, of all persons on Planet Earth, managed to score Springsteen seats could mean only one thing: the Bruce had gone the way of the Billy Joel and the Elton John. He'd been reduced to the type of troubadour *parents* go to see. Not even. He'd been reduced to the type of troubadour parents see with their families.

What Dad was suggesting seemed so dorky, so Family Channel, so . . . how shall I phrase this most succinctly? Free of charge.

When I really thought about it, turning down the chance to see Springsteen play with the E Street Band (free of charge) actually seemed sort of heretical.

After all, I'm from New Jersey.

• • •

I haven't always been from New Jersey. It is true that I was born there and spent my entire life there until high school graduation. But at various junctures, I have been from Seattle, Malibu Beach, and Australia, depending on whom I was lying to at the time.

Why the tall tales? I will tell you. From the very first time a New Jerseyan (assuming that is what we're called) meets a non–New Jerseyan, we learn that ours is a second-class state to be ridiculed and shunned. I must have been five the first time some schmuck from a *superior* state (Delaware) cracked himself up with the hilariously unpredictable question, "What exit?" When I was a teenager, the most popular character on *Saturday Night Live* was Joe Piscopo (another self-hating homeboy) doing a badly blow-dried, mildly retarded mallrat who said, "You from Joyzey? I'm from Joyzey!"

That was when I traded my gold chain for a puka-shell choker. But it wasn't until I went off to university—"off" meaning a forty-minute bus ride to NYU—that I first heard New Jerseyans referred to as "bridge-and-tunnel people." That was when I was from Australia.

As far as street cred went, Bruce was all we had. And even *he* urged us to "get out while we're young." I took his advice as soon as I was able, and settled in a city where people were raised to believe they hailed from the Hub. As opposed to the hubcap.

But this is the weird thing. The older I get, the more it seems like *every*one gets self-conscious when asked where they're from. My friend Jay grew up in Miami. "But I'm not some kind of stupid trendoid," he says defensively. "I mean, everything was really dilapidated back then. We never even went to the beach because it was so nasty. No, really." My friend Audrey is from—in chronological order—Illinois, France, Singapore, New Hampshire, Minnesota. "I used to go through the whole thing, now I just say I was born near Chicago," she told me. "The long version was way too complicated."

Some people feel like they're from every place; some like they're from no place. But at one point or another, each and every one of us must make peace with where we are from. Perhaps by going to New Jersey to see the Bruce with our family.

● ● ●

If words could describe the poignant display of Bruce bonding that transpired that evening, I would be the recipient of a Pulitzer prize. Alas, that day is not coming anytime soon. And so, I present you with the touching montage sequence that follows:

- **RICHIE,** winning the preconcert water-balloon toss, held in a parking lot designed to look like Asbury Park—complete with arcade games, Clarence Clemons karaoke, and actual sand, trucked in from down the shore. (Yes, we really say it like that.)

- **BEBE,** a Garden State girl so overcome with *joie de Jersey* that she offered—no, *demanded*—to buy the whole family commemorative, insanely overpriced concert T-shirts. (But first we had to try them on to make sure they didn't run large in the shoulders.)

- **RONALD,** his ears stuffed with cotton balls, standing on his air-cushion-insoled feet for almost all three hours of the Bruce's set, high-fiving each of us during "Born to Run."

Then there was I, who began the evening's festivities muttering something about all the home-perming, Camaro-driving, fried-dough-eating, *Bruuuuuuce*-screaming bridge-and-tunnel people—and ended up understanding the one thing these people *really* had in common: they were having a Totally Great Time. These people would never try to reinvent themselves with puka-shell chokers and crappy Crocodile Dundee accents. These people wouldn't *consider* assimilating into a constipated New England city where residents actually believed they were from the Hub of the universe. These were a proud people. These were *my* people.

I am not even kidding when I tell you I triumphantly donned my commemorative concert T-shirt during "I Came for You."

I air-guitared, also.

Also, I sang along. "I Came for You" seemed to sum up my journey, if that doesn't sound too Family Channel.

And if it does, what can I tell you? It was a Jersey thing. You wouldn't understand.

Rage Against the Massage

MR. ZHANG has a two-and-a-half-inch scuff on his left shoe that looks like a piece of asparagus. I am keenly aware of this asparagus because I've been staring at it with the pinpoint-pupiled panic normally associated with someone about to receive a vaccination. I'm stretched stomach-down on some sort of an operating table, fingers clutched to the sheets, as Mr. Zhang pummels me about the shoulder blades with his fists. My face is pressed into the hole of a padded toilet seat/guillotine, through which I am doing my best to block out the pain and focus on the asparagus.

I have come here to relax.

I've been a little tense lately, to tell you the truth. Dead-

43

line woes, money woes, a couple of woes I really don't think are any of your business—plus I spent all of last Monday driving back home from New Jersey. It took eight (8) hours to get there because the car ignition jammed—in other words *would not turn*—when I tried pulling out of a rest stop in Connecticut. Connecticut makes me tense enough without having my ignition jam there. Ninety minutes and a can of WD-40 later, it finally unjammed, just in time for rush hour(s).

I called each of my parents when I finally reached Boston, just to let them know I was alive.

Greeting from mother: "What are you talking about, Daniel! An ignition doesn't *jam!*"

Greeting from father: "Danny, what did you *do* to the ignition to make it jam?"

● ● ●

Before I hit my thirties, stress management was a particular bailiwick of mine. Whenever stress disrupted my equilibrium, I managed it with a homeopathic method known to practitioners as "the Fattie technique." The last time I smoked this technique, however, I went a little crazy. I was at a party with some friends when it occurred to me that any one of them could be wired with a secret microphone from the FBI.

This is a theory I have not entirely discounted.

I recently discussed my creeping anxiety with a very close friend (or FBI informant) who looked me in the eye and said,

"Dan, what you need is a massage." To which I replied,
"Yeah, too bad Megan is out of town." To which he
replied,

"Not from your *wife,* from a massage therapist." To
which I replied,

"Now you're making me *really* tense."

Believe it or not, I'm no stranger to this holistic health
business. I've had acupuncture. I've seen a chiropractor. I'm
on the gingko pills, for Christ's sake. But on my list of fun
things to do in life, lying naked while a stranger touches my
back is right up there with "lick bottom of bathtub."

After a week like mine, though, I would have taken a
sip from the toilet tank if someone told me it would be relaxing.

● ● ●

"Good afternoon!" she said. "Please fill out the Intake
Form and I'll be with you in a moment." Did you notice the
word "she" in that last sentence? That pronoun indicates
that the representative who greeted me at Back Plus ("You'll
melt in our hands") was female.

I know what you're thinking: This uptight dope walks
through the door and his first thought is, *Uh-oh, what if my
massage therapist turns out to be female and I become aroused?*
Incorrect. That was my first thought after phoning in my appointment the day before. (My second thought, incidentally,
was, *Uh-oh, what if it's a guy?*) As for my *current* source of
tension, it was this: a section of the Intake Form telling me
to MARK ANY AREA REQUIRING SPECIAL ATTEN-
TION ON THE DIAGRAM.

The diagram was male, judging by its broad shoulders and absence of bosoms. But there was a crucial detail missing from the diagram's personal region, if you know what I am saying here. And since my only area requiring special attention was a sore upper hip (tendinitis sustained from an eight-hour drive from New Jersey?), my marks looked like this:

Figure A: Area Requiring Special Attention

Three minutes later, I was staring at the chilling asparagus shoes of Mr. Zhang. He seemed eager to teach a lesson to the pervert with the dirty diagram.

But *four* minutes later, something weird(er) happened. I stopped fixating on his feet and began noticing his hands. There was something different about these hands. They were bigger; stronger; devoid of my wife's wedding ring. As he pounded and flogged my tension away, I realized that Mr. Zhang had the hands of my dreams. Literally. I fell asleep.

Of course I woke up when he started with my feet. One thing you should know about me is that *all* hands are forbidden on my feet, even the one wearing my wife's wedding ring. I can't even touch my *own* feet. It's not just that they creep me out, which they do, it's that I am extremely ticklish.

"No feet, Mr. Zhang," I said. "Feet, *no!*"

But that Mr. Zhang, he was a feisty one. He rubbed my ankles, had his way with my heels. And when he pulled on my pinkie toe, I do believe I let out a silly little giggle. "*I'm . . . so . . . ticklish,*" I tried to say, but it felt so good that I had to surrender. It's just us in here, I figured, and we had something special.

Words cannot describe the pleasure I experienced when Mr. Zhang took my upper hip into his powerful hands and paid special attention to it.

At that moment, I knew that Mr. Zhang wasn't the kind of guy who'd ever read anything dirty into my diagram. Mr. Zhang felt my pain. But more importantly, he made it go away.

And then, he up and walked out the door. It's not like I expected a commitment, but there was something very intimate about our little encounter. I was left naked and alone, staring at the only piece of art on the wall, entitled *Whiplash Injuries of the Head and Neck*.

"Call me!" I longed to shout out. But my time was up, and Zhangy had other backs to batter.

If there is one thing I am certain of, it is this: One day, I know I will see Mr. Zhang again. I have an appointment next Sunday at noon.

Never Mind Your Manners

LADIES AND GENTLEMEN, would we ever begin eating while the bread basket is being passed?"

"No we wouldn't!"

"Would we ever pop our dinner roll into our mouths, ladies and gentlemen, and chew-chew-chew like a little squirrel?"

"No we wouldn't!"

"Would we even *think* of buttering our entire roll at once, ladies and gentlemen?"

"No we wouldn't!"

"*Wonderful,* ladies and gentlemen. We would break off a small piece of our roll and we would butter it with the

48

small butter knife that is perched at the top of our plate, *wouldn't* we, ladies and gentlemen?"

"Yes we would!"

After several decades of practicing not exactly bad, but certainly somewhat . . . *questionable* manners, it was with great curiosity that I went to "An Afternoon of Etiquette," led by Leona Wolcott of the Leona Wolcott School of Social Sophistication. All I told Miss Leona, as she requested to be called, was that I'd be attending her seminar as a freelance reporter, which was true, to an extent. (The extent to which I could write it off as a business expense on this year's tax return.) But even truer was that I'd be attending as a guy who just last week caught himself belching *and* loud-yawning in a movie theater and a subway car, respectively; who always forgets to put the napkin on his lap; who has become increasingly bewildered by all the forks.

Who could have predicted that these would be concerns I'd one day be embarrassed by? I used to think only the boring were well behaved, and that being socially savvy meant never having an affair preceded by the word "formal." But life, it is a crazy roller-coaster ride of endless twists and turns. Today I am the co-owner of good silver, and a frequent attendee at the kind of business functions where funnel-shots are frowned upon.

At first I planned to take Miss Leona's seminar for young professionals, but it seemed geared to those already comfortable acting in what is known as an age-appropriate manner. I selected, instead, her remedial class, an all-day occasion open to children ages eight to twelve. I figured I'd fit right in.

Miss Leona was teaching the kids a thing or two about floral arrangement when I arrived. Her venue was a meeting room at one of the city's upper-crustiest hotels, dolled up for the day by a banquet table set for ten. Based on her appearance, I put her between thirty-five and seventy years of age. She was one of those waxen-looking women who was so perfectly put together with her navy pinstripe suit and her shiny pulled-back hair and her completely exfoliated self that it was really impossible to tell. Her disposition, predictably, was equally polished.

"Welcome! I was worried you got lost," she gushed when I first walked in. By the time I left, I knew this was just her way of saying something else: "I am pissed that you're late."

As for my fellow participants, they were pretty much what you'd expect from a demographic whose parents could blow 275 bucks on etiquette lessons. Ten fancypants children with names such as Clayton, Marianna, Park. But besides the class distinctions, the only factors that separated me from them were (a) they were *real* children, and (b) they seemed a lot more mature than me. Though I did immediately hit it off with this one kid, Nick, a ten-something renegade who made the radical fashion statement of wearing *his* light-blue Oxford button-down shirt *un*tucked. Nick struck me as the kind of kid who's going to get kicked out of Choate in ten years for dealing. I knew we'd be good friends when he wrapped his napkin around his head during the lesson on "fan-folding."

"Nick, honey, I'd like you to go ahead and remove that napkin from your head and place it on your lap, where it belongs. Do it *now,* darling," Miss Leona said with her simulated smile. She was about to offer counsel on olive-pit management, and by now it was clear she had her teacher's pets. Nick wasn't one of them. Whitney was. Never in all my years have I met a nine-year-old so good at sucking up as Whitney. When we all had to go around the room talking about our flower arrangements, Whitney said she was trying to model hers after the type of thing she imagined Miss Leona herself might create. (When it was Nick's turn, he said—and I quote—"I'm not really into flower arranging." I had to echo his sentiments when called upon to deconstruct my own wilting clump of stems.) Nick and I decided to sit next to each other when lunchtime—I mean "luncheon time"—rolled around. That was probably my first mistake (after arriving twelve minutes late), as it indicated to Miss Leona that I'd fallen in with the wrong crowd.

About the meal itself, let me just say that you don't know the meaning of the word "privileged" until you've seen a distinguished, middle-aged gentleman in a dinner jacket serving chicken marsala to a table full of guests whose feet do not reach the ground. Our four-course feast began with drink orders. Whitney ordered a Diet Coke, proving it's never too soon for waifish nine-year-olds to be on diets. Then again, every little girl at the table ordered a diet something—everyone except Jennifer, that is, who politely requested a chocolate milk, straight up with a straw. Jennifer had a refreshing, childlike vulnerability about her. I first detected it when she raised her hand and asked if she might be excused to go to the ladies' room.

"Oh, sweetheart, I'm sorry," Miss Leona replied, pouting her lips into a sad face. "But I promise we'll get to that later. We like to go in groups."

We *do*? I thought. But what did I know? An hour earlier, I was still the kind of dirtbag who buttered his entire dinner roll at once and chew-chew-chewed it like a little squirrel.

With our first course came a question. "Now, ladies and gentlemen," Miss Leona inquired, "what is the first thing one does when presented with this *scrumptious* shrimp cocktail appetizer?"

For me, the obvious answer was: one eats it. If one grew up in the Zevin household, one recalled that table manners boiled down to consuming whatever was put in front of one in as rapid and loud a manner as possible.

"This dish I made from scratch!" my mother, donning her trademark *Kiss Me, I'm The Chef!* apron, would announce, meaning she had microwaved a frozen brick of Jolly Green Giant spinach soufflé as opposed to serving takeout from Hunan Wok. If it was a formal occasion, where relatives were invited, polite dinner conversation centered not so much on the food as on the process by which it was digested.

"Spinach?! I can't eat spinach! I'll get loose doody!" Aunt Sandy would yell across the table.

"Well, in that case, you should be eating my pilaf! It's binding!" Mom would bark back, plunking down a bowl of Uncle Ben's.

"Don't give her the rice! She gets all blocked up from the rice!" Uncle Mickey would chime in, brandishing a turkey leg for emphasis before delivering his traditional discourse on the powers of prune juice.

So it was really one of those small moments of enlightenment to learn that the first thing one does when one is presented with a *scrumptious* shrimp cocktail appetizer is to not eat it. In fact, a gentleman mustn't eat anything until his hostess has taken the first bite—another move that wouldn't fly at the Zevins', since it would be met by the hostess with the following reaction: "Daniel! Why aren't you eating my spinach soufflé?! What, you don't *like* it?!"

Once your hostess has taken the first bite of the *scrumptious* shrimp cocktail appetizer, this is your cue to operate your silverware using your "power fingers." Miss Leona called on Whitney to demonstrate, surprise, surprise. The rest of us watched as Whitney followed her blow-by-blow instructions to open her palm, place her shrimp fork between her thumb and index finger, turn her hand over, place her index (a/k/a "power") finger firmly on the handle of her shrimp fork, use her other hand to repeat the procedure with her shrimp knife, pierce the part of the shrimp meat closest to her with the shrimp fork, slice off half with the shrimp knife—*making sure to use her power fingers to keep everything firmly in place*—place her shrimp knife down on her plate with the tip at twelve noon, switch her shrimp fork into the hand that previously held her shrimp knife, and slowly bring it "up-up-up" to her mouth.

Whitney power-fingered flawlessly, but I noticed my buddy Nick lost the thread somewhere around the twelve noon part. He was clutching his fork and knife in his fists, desperately trying to hack off a piece of scrumptious shrimp cocktail appetizer. It looked like the little guy was about to cry. I told him not to sweat it; that, sometimes, even grown-ups just grab a couple of shrimps by the backside and shove 'em into their mouths. But just as I was about to show him how, I was interrupted.

"*Yoo-hoo,* Mr. Dan . . ." It was Miss Leona, using the passive-aggressive singsongy voice I had grown to despise. "Elbows, Mr. Dan, *el-*bows . . ."

By this point, I felt like flipping Miss Leona my own private power finger. I don't know if it was just that I was a few years older than the other kids or what, but I got the distinct feeling she'd been using me as her whipping boy all day. Like when I asked Marianna to pass the salt. Miss Leona shot me the stink-eye and said, "Ladies and gentlemen, did you know that grown-up people who take business meals often won't hire someone who salts his food before tasting it? Pre-salting shows poor judgment, *doesn't* it, ladies and gentlemen?" A little later, I dropped one of my spoons. Waiting until the precise moment I was bent over my seat trying to pick it up, she commented, "We *never* pick up our spoon when it drops on the floor, *do* we, ladies and gentlemen. If we are well mannered, we wait for our *waiter* to pick it up."

But the thing that made her the craziest was definitely the elbows. When it came to elbow surveillance, it wasn't just me she was watching. Miss Leona was like a hawk, coasting casually along until swooping down to startle her prey.

"As we see, we must write our thank-you notes no more than three days after receiving our—*Timothy! I think I may see your elbows on the table, but who knows? Maybe you're just trying to protect your food from theft."*

"If our tea is piping hot, we do not blow on it to make it—*Now, Park, what are we going to DO with those little elbows of yours? Hmm? Sweetheart?*"

I think it was while she was diagramming the various components of a salmon fillet that I noticed Nick had propped one of his elbows up on the table. I kicked him under the table, frightened that my new best friend was in jeopardy of being next unless he took swift measures to rectify the situation. Alas, I was too late, and out came the most macabre elbow caveat yet.

"Nick, darling, I can't ever send you home if you keep your elbows on the table, now *can* I?"

"Then I guess I'll be staying here all night!" Nick replied, fearlessly. The girls gasped. The boys broke out into fits of giggles. I myself nearly spit out my tea, but that, of course, would have been discourteous. And God only knows what Miss Leona would have done to my tongue.

"Nick, Nick, Nick . . ." said Miss Leona, smiling. "Aren't you *funny,* darling?" She issued forth her familiar fake laugh—the kind that becomes a cackle in scary movies, always leading to a close-up of the villain's tonsils.

• • •

Question and Answer Period came after dessert, a fancy fruit tart and sorbet situation that Miss Leona made us eat European style, which had something to do with "escorting" it into our mouths. The first question came from Jennifer, who once again asked if she could use the ladies' room.

Once again, her request was denied. Then there was Miss Leona's deeply weird response to Clayton's excellent question, "What do you do if you hate the food you've been served?"

"*Darling,*" she replied in a newly acquired British accent. "You can't hate something that can't hate you back."

"But *why* can't you hate something that can't hate you back?" Clayton persisted.

"Because, *darling,* eggplant doesn't have a soul."

And with that cryptic assertion, Miss Leona smugly returned to her easel to tackle the biggies:

- food caught in teeth
- belch/sneeze/cough
- parents yelling

Far and away, belch/sneeze/cough was the standout subject, with "belch" eliciting the greatest interest from everyone, including myself. It was truly impressive how much these kids yearned for knowledge about belching. "What if it's a really long belch?" "What if you try to hold it in and it comes out your nose?" "What if you belch on the subway?" (I didn't have the balls to ask this one myself. Nick agreed to do it for me.) Miss Leona had a standard line on the whole belching arena: Try to keep your lips together, and don't draw a lot of attention to it. I made a mental note.

After belching, I found it interesting that "parents yelling" was the runner-up topic, suggesting that maybe these kids didn't hail from such genteel households after all. They wanted to know what to do when their parents were fighting in a restaurant, fighting at a friend's house, fighting at a friend's house with the friends. Miss Leona, who was becoming uncharacteristically fidgety, finally put the kibosh on the subject with another standard line: Don't get involved in the argument. Just excuse yourself to go to the bathroom.

Jennifer immediately shot up her hand.

"I have to go to the bathroom *now*," she said.

Miss Leona complied, finally, saving herself the trouble of adding a whole new component to the curriculum:

* wetting self at banquet table

I would have to say that one of the most memorable moments of the day was when Miss Leona drew the following portrait on her easel:

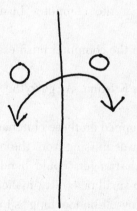

Now what in the hell is this? I wondered. *The deranged scribblings of an aspiring cult leader? A desperate cry for help?* Well, yes, obviously, but also it was her depiction of The Art of

Small Talk. Small talk, explained Miss Leona, was like volleyball (hence the illustrated balls). When you meet someone new at a birthday party, for instance, the idea is to volley back and forth with "small" topics, lobbing questions to your partner in a manner that will make them think you have some kind of authentic interest in them. Politics, religion, and war are not appropriate topics for small talk. Movies, bands, TV, family, and sports are. It was then that I realized my entire conversational scope is limited to small talk.

The group paired off to practice, and nearly every conversation went something like this:

"It is a pleasure to meet you. Do you have any hobbies?"

"Yes, I like horseback riding. How about you?"

"I like lacrosse. What does your father do?"

"He works in the computer business. How about yours?"

"He works in the computer business. Who is your best friend at school?"

"Her name is Kristina. We go to the same country club. How about you?"

As I eavesdropped on these chitchat lessons, I felt like something major was missing from the mix. It was the one subject even total strangers could bond over; the cornerstone of *grown-up* small talk: dirty, malicious gossip. I envisioned Nick and myself hobnobbing as follows:

"It is a pleasure to meet you. Do you think Miss Leona has ever been laid?"

"No way, how about you?"

"I think she has the hots for that scheming Whitney with the sparkly makeup on her cheeks. How about you?"

"I think Whitney likes the dude with the bowl haircut who couldn't work his tea strainer. How about you?"

"I think I'd like to get out of here already. How about you?"

"Yes, I would very much like to go smoke a joint in the boys' room. How about you?"

• • •

Shortly before we all received our end-of-the-day gift bags of sample-sized hand lotion, hair conditioner, and mouthwash, a terribly shy little girl wearing pigtails and clunky glasses raised her hand. She'd barely said a word all afternoon but clearly had something to get off her chest before we were finally released.

"Um, okay, like . . . okay," she stammered. "I guess what I wanted to know was, is it *ever* okay to have bad manners?"

Miss Leona raised one eyebrow in a *Mommie Dearest* kind of way. Earnestly, the little girl pressed on.

"Okay, like, let's say you're at a sleepover at your friend's house and you're all in a tent in the backyard and you're, like, eating pizza and having fun and stuff. Is it okay to, like, not sit up straight?"

Here, verbatim, was Miss Leona's response:

"Well, taking into consideration that it's probably a group of six or so girls, and you're so excited to be with your friends, and you're out in the backyard and you're probably sitting cross-legged on the ground and you're leaning in, and you're not in a normal position of sitting in a chair, probably the body's normal reaction would be to lean forward to get into a comfortable position. And many times, ladies and gentlemen, a comfortable position is supporting your head by resting your hand on your leg, and you're right—that *isn't* perfect posture, but I would say it can be acceptable in a situation such as that."

• • •

Have you ever wondered where repression comes from? Have you ever wondered what produces all the horribly inhibited, perfectly proper people that you never really get to know because they never really let their guards down, not even at a sleepover where everyone is, like, eating pizza and having fun and stuff? Ever since attending "An Afternoon of Etiquette," I've decided that maybe what happened to some of those people is that, at a very early age, they were introduced to the Miss Leonas of the world who always made them think twice before deciding it's okay to slouch in a friend's tent, and who not only referred to them as "ladies and gentlemen" but expected them to *be* ladies and gentlemen, even though they were really "girls and boys" who already had enough to figure out without the added anxieties of acceptable elbow placement.

That is why I'm launching my own etiquette seminar for youngsters. It will be called Mr. Dan's Day of Social Disgrace, and it will feature instruction on food fights, fart technique, and picking your nose and eating it! It will be rooted in the founding principle that if a child needs to urinate, he or she will not only be allowed, but encouraged to do so. And twenty years later, if that child should become a grown-up who has recently caught himself belching *and* loud-yawning in a movie theater and a subway car, respectively; or who always forgets to put the napkin on his lap; or who has become increasingly bewildered by all the forks, he is not going to care. Because, thanks to Mr. Dan, he will have learned something more important than the fact that some people will judge him based on his breeding. He will have learned not to give a rat's ass.

Confession:

"The future freaks me out."

Don't Plan on It

I T WASN'T THAT I planned to meet Jeffrey and Shelly for soft-serve frozen yogurt; it was that they planned to meet me. They planned when we'd meet, where we'd meet, even which Far-Out Featured Flavor we'd have (Faux Cocoa, Raisinette mix-ins, waffle cone). And as we ate our yogurt, they discussed their plans.

They planned to be out of their place on September fifteenth. It was crazy to keep paying rent when they could be building long-term equity by owning, and since they'd stuck to their plan of putting $550 a month into their joint account, they could afford this funky loft downtown that was cheap now but was guaranteed to go through the roof in five to seven years. At that point, they planned to sell it and move to Vermont, where the schools would be better for the kids, the female of which they had last year, the male of which (fingers crossed!) they planned to have next year, after Shelly finished her residency and Jeffrey started his design studio. He never planned to stay in his current job more than two years anyway.

Also, they have converted to the Roth IRA.

When I grow up, I plan to be just like Jeffrey and Shelly. Right now, I'm just a little jealous. They are directed, focused, goal-oriented. They don't sit around and wait for opportunity to knock, they march over to opportunity's apartment and lean on the buzzer until it answers the door. These two have a master plan. These two are master planners.

Whenever I see these two, I feel compelled to plan more. If I was like Jeffrey and Shelly, I start thinking, I would have gotten my taxes in on time instead of paying the penalty fee again. I would have an assistant by now, or at least sired a couple of kids to help out around the house. I would *certainly* have converted to the Roth IRA, which *is* something I plan on converting to as soon as I find out what it is. Which I will do this week. Yes. By the end of this week, I am going to find out what the Roth IRA is. I may not actually *convert* to the Roth IRA. That, I plan to do another time, such as *next* week. But this week, I will find out what it is.

There. I have a plan. I feel much better now.

• • •

Perhaps you have deduced that I'm not one of your master planners. I'm one of your minor planners. Notice I didn't say I'm one of your under-planners. Your under-planners are your Be Here Now, Live in the Moment, la-la-hey-hey, *whatever* type of individuals who are just chillin' at the folk festival until they wake up to discover they've become elderly osteoporosis sufferers who never bothered to sign up for Medicare.

Your minor planners, on the other hand, exercise just enough foresight to ensure that we never, under any circumstances, turn into your under-planners. We're not so hot with long-term plans, but we're skilled with short-term planettes. Most of these revolve around two areas of interest:

1. where our next check is coming from
2. where we'll be spending it over the weekend

As for your master planners, they don't worry about the weekend. They already have plans. They are working on their wills.

But enough about them. What kind of planner are *YOU*? Before reading further, set some time aside and plan to take . . .

The Zevin Planning Aptitude Test (ZPAT)

1. The way I wound up in my current occupation was by:

(a) answering an ad   (b) starting a multinational systems integration conglomeration   (c) occu-what?

2. Which of the following items would most likely appear on your "to-do" list?

(a) get cream cheese   (b) get married   (c) get "to-do" list

3. Fill in the blank. "By the time I'm seventy, I plan to
_____"

(a) convert to the Roth IRA   (b) run for reelection
(c) get my driver's license

If you are unable to recognize your planning profile from the survey above, you are probably a master planner. It's just that you're too embarrassed to admit it, much like my friend Keith, who resides in the city of New York on a tightly synchronized schedule dictated by a computerized device called a—let me steady myself before I type the next two words—Palm Pilot.

I'm not talking some namby-pamby Filofax here. I'm talking the deluxe mothership model, with the one beep that tells you it's a month before your staff meeting, the other beep that tells you it's six days until your haircut, the acoustical "Happy Birthday to You" beep that tells you when to send someone a card, the electronic beeping book edition of *Fodor's New York* to help plan your trip to the card store, the preprogrammable, 365-disc-a-day CD player so you'll always know what you'll be listening to whenever you're not listening to beeps, and the microscreen, cable-ready TV, providing round-the-clock coverage of the extended AccuWeather five-year forecast.

Recently, I asked Keith what he wanted to do when he came up for one of his impromptu visits (twenty-one-day advance purchase required; blackout dates apply).

"You know me," he said. "No plans."

• • •

On the one hand, people like Keith are just kidding themselves when they say no plans. On the other, people like me are just kidding *our*selves when we make mean-spirited, hyperbolic remarks regarding their Palm Pilots. Because here's what I *really* think whenever Keith whips out that Palm Pilot: Why don't *I* have one of those?

I will tell you why. Because of the brew pub. Let me elaborate. I have been thinking of opening my own brew pub ever since getting my first fake ID at age seventeen. I am thinking about it right now, as a matter of fact. But *now*, only one sentence later, I am thinking: Who knows where I'll be living next year? If I open a brew pub, when will I ever travel the world? And if I travel the world, where will I get the money to come back home? Maybe I can just sublet a brew pub over the summer and see how it goes. Who wants to spend the summer in a brew pub? What if it's a beach day? What if I miss something at the brew pub while I'm off at the beach? Hmm . . . I wonder what movies are playing at the Kendall Theater this weekend.

• • •

How much simpler life would be if I were a master planner! I would get my oil changed every three months or 3,000 miles, whichever came first. I would plant bulbs in the fall to blossom in the spring. Never again would I arrive at the Elliott Smith show to discover it was sold out even though Jeffrey and Shelly bought their tickets three months in advance.

I would have asked Stacy Borinsky to the senior prom before Allen Lowe did, if I were a master planner. I would be talking to you from my own brew pub right now. I would be writing these words on a Palm Pilot. With pride.

If I were a master planner, I would have a step-by-step program to achieve my goals and get exactly what I want out of life.

Which, unfortunately, would entail *knowing* exactly what I want out of life.

I've been planning to tackle that one for a few decades now, but lately I've been wondering what to do if I never figure it out. I guess it's time to start thinking about a backup plan.

Confession:

"I have turned into a 'pet person.' "

Where the Dogs Are

NOT TO BRAG, but I roused myself out of bed every day this week at five o'clock (A.M.). Relax. I haven't turned into one of those rise-n'-shinin', decaf-drinkin', Weather Channel–watchin', homicidal-urge-inducin' morning people.

I have, however, turned into one of the dog people.

The dog people are the people who gather at dawn to throw saliva-soaked tennis balls around parks nationwide. A while ago, I wouldn't have said they were my kind of crowd, as five A.M. was frankly not an hour with which I had much familiarity. But a while ago, I didn't have Chloe, the orphaned Lab mutt who appeared frisky—as opposed to frenzied—when she first conned me into taking her home from the pound. To say that Chloe's internal alarm clock goes off

68

at five A.M. would be misleading, because it would suggest that she requires sleep. In fact, she requires Ritalin. Either that or forty minutes each morning with the dog people.

I feel very close to the dog people, though I do not know any of their names. We remember only the dogs' names, you see. As for *our* identities, we're just "Chloe's father," "Augie's mother," or "Sadie's parents," to name but a few. Our mission is the same: to chuck the tennis ball until Chloe, Augie, Sadie, and the rest collapse from acute canine exhaustion so they'll spend the remainder of the day sleeping (or, in Chloe's case, "resting") rather than dining on our speaker wires.

The only time it is permissible to stop chucking the ball is when one of the dogs needs a time-out to "poop." Canine excrement, I have learned, is referred to only as "poop" by the dog people. I once made the mistake of using a more colorful term, and was met by stunned silences all around.

But now that I've got the lingo straight, the other dog people and I talk every morning. We don't small-talk, either. We engage in the kind of deep, meaningful conversation you can only have with someone else who is outdoors at five o'clock (A.M.) using a plastic Star Market bag to pick up a pile of dogshit. Poop, I mean.

"Hmm, looks like Chloe has diarrhea again," I proclaim.

"Yes, I see what you mean," Augie's mother concurs. "Must be eating too much grass."

"Sadie ate a washcloth last night," interjects her father. "Vomited it up like a Super Ball."

I cannot emphasize enough the significance of these

morning chats. With each discussion of Sadie's swollen anal sacs or Augie's weakness for squirrels, I feel a little more connected; a little less like the only father in the city whose daughter does not come every time (okay, *any* time) she is called. Who else but the dog people would have clued me into the Drs. Foster and Smith catalogue, featuring hickory-smoked Choo-Hooves at rock-bottom prices? Where else but at the dog field would I have learned that, when it comes to problem "hot spots," the guck from an aloe plant is nature's alternative to cortisone cream. We are all about support and sharing and honesty. Show us a playground full of *real* parents and we will make them look like amateurs.

• • •

One evening I saw one of the dog people at the Sir Speedy copy shop I go to. We were both without our dogs. We looked at each other in that fleeting way people do when they think they know each other but aren't really sure. Then it occurred to me: Sadie's mother! What was she getting copied? Where does she live? Has she seen any good movies lately? Both of us stood there stupidly by the lamination machine until I finally decided to break the ice.

"Uh, how is your dog?" I said.

• • •

It took a long time to find the canine clique that felt right to Chloe and me. In my neighborhood alone, there were three major scenes going on. We started at Fresh Pond Park, where most of the dogs seemed like they just came out of the Westminster Kennel Club, and most of their mothers and fathers seemed like they just came out of the Harvard Faculty Club. The dog people there didn't really throw the tennis ball as much as they stood around observing the animals' behavioral responses with regard to retrieval-avoidance pack interaction. Plus, a woman with a giant black poodle named *Margaret* asked me—swear on a stack of Drs. Foster and Smith catalogues—if Chloe "has a problem with ethnic diversity."

Chloe, at the time, was barking at this guy who happened to be black. I immediately experienced that familiar self-consciousness that only we dog people understand: the sense that strangers are passing judgment on us based upon our dog's behavior. *What has Chloe's father been telling her about people of color to make his dog so prejudiced?* Margaret's mother was obviously thinking about me. I felt ashamed, though I knew the truth: Chloe was barking because the guy had a tennis ball.

The dog people at Danehy Park were an entirely different breed. This was the salt-of-the-earth dog scene, and rarely did we see anyone with a purebred anything here, much less a poodle named Margaret. Danehy doggie mothers and fathers just chucked a few balls until they finished their cigarettes, then went home and got ready for work. The couple of times I actually spoke to any of them, we covered the customary subject of effluvia, of course, but they all seemed preoccupied with the man I've come to call "the bad guy."

From what I gathered, the bad guy is some sort of official canine cop who protects parks from the threat of dogs that are not properly licensed. According to Bo's mother, who was holding a load in a CVS bag at the time, the bad guy also issues fines to dog people whose pets are "off-leash." I split this scene pronto, worried that I'd be booked on two counts: unleashed and unlicensed.

And so it was that I stumbled upon my doggie scene of choice: a lesser-known softball field abutting a parking lot and a graffiti-covered grammar school. We're a misfit bunch, Sadie's parents, Augie's mom, and me, but we are going to be the next big thing, I tell you. Why, just this morning we were joined by a potential new member—Rocket's mother—who found herself displaced when the Tufts football field was closed off to canines (surely by decree of the bad guy). I'm amazed at how well I got to know her in the forty minutes we spent chucking the ball and picking up poop. For example, Rocket has ear mites, is scared of luggage, and likes to sleep in the bathtub.

I hope she (and her son) will be back tomorrow, and will one day become permanent members of our little scene. For we are the dog people, and everyone is welcome. Everyone except the bad guy.

Not My Junior Year Abroad

WHEN MY YOUNGER brother, Richie, told me he'd be spending a semester of college studying in Madrid, I sat him down and posed a serious question: When could I visit? My own erstwhile semester abroad was one of those quintessential turning points where horizons are broadened, identities are shaped, Nutella is eaten. I was young, free, and boarding with Mr. and Mrs. Knud Ølaf-Schmidt of Copenhagen, Denmark. Scandinavia seemed like the perfect place for student exchange, not because I had any idea where it was on a map, but because my friend, Hal, went the semester before and said the girls there were the "foxiest."

Fifteen years later, I longed to catch up with Richie at this critical juncture in *his* life. I would spend one reckless week in Spain, showing an amateur how it's really done. What follows are the often enlightening, always disturbing, heavily edited excerpts from my travel journals, then and now.

Semester Abroad, Copenhagen, 20 Years of Age

This is gonna be *the* most intense semester. Last night, me, Keith, Sari, Cathy, Erik Daner, Jeff, Tim, Denise, Bjorn, Bjorn's friend whose name I'm spacing out on, and this chick Megan from my Danish Literature class (cute + smart = probably has boyfriend) stayed out *all night* (4:30 A.M.) drinking Tuborg Øl at this pub only the Danish students know about and then today, me, Tim, Bill, Cathy, and Denise went to the Hamlet castle and took a train to the Louisiana, which is definitely the coolest museum I've ever seen, and tonight we're all going back to that jazz club we went to last Thursday where everyone was all boho wearing gloves with cut-out finger holes and smoking and everything. I am sooooooo stoked! My Eurail Pass came in the mail today! When I opened the envelope it was like this huge metaphor of me having the "whole world in my hands."

Week Abroad, Madrid, 35 Years of Age

I cannot see out of my right eye. I'm on the bed in our hotel room with a gauze pad the size of a pancake on my *ojo*. Megan and I landed a few hours ago, and when Richie met us at the airport, he had an elaborate itinerary planned—a tapas lunch, a tour of the Prado, the old city, the new city, the middle-aged city, sangria, paella, piñatas, cucarachas, the whole tour de force or however you say it in Spanish. The one thing he didn't plan for was that my cornea would have a brush with some shrubbery a few hours before takeoff. I was trying to get Chloe's tennis ball out of a bush in the backyard before dropping her off at the dog-sitter's. Ten hours later, I stumbled off the plane in Madrid, wearing these mirrored, Erik Estrada–esque sunglasses I bought at the airport. I think Richie figured I was trying to be cool, as opposed to trying to conceal the gruesome, swollen mass that used to be my eye. I hated to disappoint him since we haven't hung out since seeing the Bruce last summer, but when I removed my *CHiPs* apparatus, it was clear he'd have to revise our itinerary. First, he needed to find me an ophthalmologist. *Then* we'd rage all night.

I just realized I haven't checked out our minibar.

Minibar sucks. Three on a scale of one to ten, from what I could tell with my good eye. Plus, everything in there has this weird orange tint, which I keep forgetting is just from the horrible orange drops the Spanish doctor squirted into my pupils this afternoon. Richie managed to get me to a clinic, and as I tried to tell the doctor—who didn't speak English— what happened, I realized I have zero retention of all the Spanish I ever took in school. All I remember are these useless sayings we had to memorize in ninth grade. *En boca cerrada no entran moscas* ("Flies don't enter a closed mouth"). *Perros que ladran no muerden* ("Barking dogs don't bite"). Luckily, Richie was able to relay my condition in rapid-fire Español. He said, "*Mi hermano Daniél babababababababababababababababa.*" Likely translation: "My brother Dan is trying to recapture his youth by crashing my junior semester abroad. I am sure that even you, a Spanish ophthalmologist, can appreciate the irony of rushing him in for medical attention as soon as he arrives."

"Tell him I keep getting this crud in it," I told Richie. "It's like pus or something."

"*Mi hermano tiene . . . uh,* poos," Richie translated. Guess he's not so fluent after all.

"*Si, señor,* poos," the doctor replied, much to the delight of wife and brother alike. I've been here less than a day and already I've earned the nickname "Señor Poos."

Besides the horrible orange eyedrops that have tinted my vision, the Spanish ophthalmologist gave me a box of tea. If Richie has his translation straight, I am not supposed to drink the tea. I am supposed to rinse my eyes with the tea, every four to six hours. Which reminds me. It's nine P.M. Tea time. Richie and Megan went out for tapas a little while ago, but I was sound asleep. Megan woke me up before they left. She said, "Adiós, Señor Poos." Richie cracked up.

Let them have their little laugh. Tonight, I'll rinse with Spanish eye-tea and go to bed. But tomorrow, I'll be livin' *la vida loca*!

I wonder if we get free HBO in this hotel.

Semester Abroad

Backpacking through Europe is *the* most intense thing I've ever done in my whole life. Me, Keith, Erik, Denise, Megan (❤), Sari, Tim, and Jeff got to Venice last night and all the youth hostels were totally booked so we looked through *Let's Go Europe!* for other places and it said you're allowed to sleep outside on the steps of the train station (that book rocks!!) so everyone's like, "Excellent!" and we rolled out our sleeping bags and played quarters, which Megan called "liras" (❤❤), till everyone finally passed out (3:30 A.M. or *later*).

Week Abroad

Today I was forced to walk on the shady side of the street all afternoon as my eye has developed an excruciating sensitivity to light. My new system is to wear my Erik Estrada sunglasses outdoors and a backup pair of lightly tinted rose-colored spectacles indoors. It's especially trippy to wear the rose ones inside since everything is already orange from the horrible eyedrops. Combined, all the interiors of Madrid take on this freaky brownish glow. Not that we're seeing many interiors of Madrid. No matter what time of day we walk around, everything is closed for *siesta*. How anyone can sleep on these crappy beds all day is beyond me. We're paying $200 a night, and our room has two singles with mattresses stuffed with concrete. Not that I'm complaining. I learned a long time ago that travel isn't about comfort, it's about experience. You've got to focus on the positive!

The weather in Madrid is *spectacular*. Sunny and warm all day. Hot, actually. I thought I was gonna sweat to death in that park Richie schlepped us to this afternoon. He had this idea that we'd just sit in the sun and have a beer. He meant well, but he isn't quite grasping the fact that exposure to light triggers an intense, searing pain in my cerebellum. I sat in the shade and had a bottled water. That's the thing about travel: you gotta hydrate.

Went to the Reina Sofia after the park. There was a Picasso retrospective covering everything from his blue period to his rose period. Of course, it all looked like one freaky brownish period to me. Richie's gotten really into art history. He said he's been to the museum once a week since his semester began. I can understand why. It was, like, the first place all week with decent air conditioning. Megan almost bought some *Guernica* coasters in the gift shop. But then she had a coughing fit and decided to rest up at the hotel. I'm worried that her cold is turning into swollen glands.

Semester Abroad

The most intense thing I've been contemplating is how totally cool it is that Danes, unlike Americans, don't get uptight over people who are nonconformists. There's this part of Copenhagen called Christiania where *everything* is legal. Today, me, Keith, Tim, Erik Daner, Big Joe, Cathy, Sari, and Denise went over there to check it out. You can go up to anyone and buy *primo* hash and it's totally allowed. We partied with some Danish dude who kept calling me Spicoli from *Fast Times at Ridgemont High,* which is so weird that they even *got* that movie in Europe, but then I told him I really *was* Sean Penn and he believed me and he asked for my autograph, so I signed his forehead!! That was *the* most baked I've ever been in my whole life. . . .

Week Abroad

I have reached my limit re: the Spaniard/smoking situation. As I write this, we're on the high-speed train to Seville, a/k/a the Ashtray Express. Even with my protective Erik Estrada eyegear, I can feel the cigarette smoke seeping into my cornea, mixing with my *poos,* leading to certain blindness. Megan has been wheezing since we boarded. Great, I'll get to Seville in need of a glass eye and she'll need a respirator. Good thing Richie's still with us so he can find another emergency room. How is it that he seems completely un-aware of the poor air quality on this train? He's just sitting there listening to his Discman, staring at the countryside out the window. He didn't even bring any luggage. What's he gonna wear? I guess he can borrow something of mine, con-sidering that we are in possession of:

- 1 large rolling suitcase (best investment of my life)
- 1 small rolling suitcase (second best)
- 1 mid-sized canvas duffel
- 1 bike messenger bag
- 2 daypacks
- 1 auxiliary Le Sportsac shoulder tote circa 1983 cleverly stuffed into small rolling suitcase for later storage of souvenirs, and . . .
- 0 souvenirs—not counting one (1) box of Spanish eye-tea—owing to fact that all stores are closed at all times for all-day siesta

Semester Abroad

NEIL YOUNG = GOD. I've been cranking *Live Rust* on my Walkman every night before bed for like the past two weeks. ". . . All in a dream, all in a dream . . ."

Week Abroad

Last night Megan had a dream that the tile guy screwed up our bathroom floor at home. I've been a bit concerned about it myself all week. It's not that I mind him working in our house while we're in Spain, it's that I know he wasn't listening when I told him to order semiglazed, not glazed. If that guy uses glazed, he's dead.

Semester Abroad

Epiphanies of the day:
1. Success = freedom
2. I am in love with Megan (❤❤❤❤) from Danish Literature class
3. I don't ever want to go back home

Week Abroad

*Fax tile guy from hotel in Seville: SEMI-glazed.

Semester Abroad

It's Carnival week in Dope-n-hagen!! The whole city is buzzing with music and tons of tourists and parades and stuff, so a few hours ago, me, Megan, Tucker from Georgia, Bob, Erik Daner, Keith, Sari, Denise, Tim, Ingrid, Little Joe, Big Joe, Gigi, and her foxxxxxxxxy Danish sister (*not* as foxy as Megan) met at Tivoli Garden and got our faces painted and chilled out playing Frisbee and Hacky Sack and now we're off to see DIRE STRAITS, which is truly the coolest, since MARK KNOPFLER = GOD (also Neil Young).

Week Abroad

By all indications, we have chosen the single busiest week of the year to visit Seville. It's called Semana Santa—Easter week—and the entire European Union has jammed into the streets to celebrate (and smoke). I remember the travel agent said that's why she had a hard time finding a hotel, but I figured, Easter shmeester—a few eggs, a chocolate rabbit, how bad could it be? Answer: *Muy, muy* bad. Most of the roads are blocked off for these religious parades where everyone dresses up like Klansmen in the white sheets and the pointy hats, and they carry these huge floats depicting the Crucifixion of Christ. The whole thing is making me jittery. I'm no history scholar (understatement of the year), but I do remember a little something called the Spanish Inquisition . . .

Richie, of course, keeps saying how lucky we are to be here for such a major cultural event. He still hasn't learned that when it comes to major cultural events, a little goes a long way. Yesterday, it was interesting. Today, it's claustrophobic. What does he know anyway? He didn't even bring socks.

On the plus side, we finally found a pitcher of sangria that doesn't taste like Hi-C. Megan figured out that what you have to do is order a bottle of red wine with it, then you add the wine to the sangria so it's not so weak. They really don't know how to make it here.

Semester Abroad

At midnight movies tonight, me and Megan (❤❤❤❤❤) saw *the* most wicked pisser film ever made. It's called *Harold and Maude* and it's about this geekazoid kid who falls in love with this old lady but the true meaning of it is that you can do whatever you want in life which sounds so simple but SIM-PLICITY = TRUTH. Cat Stevens did the soundtrack. There's this one song that goes, "If you wanna sing out, sing out, and if you wanna be free, be free . . ."

Week Abroad

Richie brought us to this flamenco bar where people in the crowd just get up on stage and start singing spontaneously. It was fun even though it didn't start until midnight, like the rest of this country. Megan and I took a nap so we'd be able to stay up late. The weird thing was that Richie didn't make any of his smart-alec cracks about it. At first it was a relief but now it's bothering me because it means he just takes for granted that we're the kind of couple who have to take a nap in order to stay up late. Where does he come up with this stuff? I told him we were just immersing ourselves in the culture by experiencing the traditional all-day siesta.

Before we left for the bar, I figured I'd rinse with my Spanish eye-tea. I don't know what came over me, but the next thing I knew, I took a sip. I've been wondering all week what the stuff really is. Now I am reasonably certain it is chamomile.

When we got to the bar, it was packed with locals of every age. The man sitting next to us had to be eighty, but all night long, he was belting out tunes like one of the Gipsy Kings. I swear he nearly inspired me to get up on stage myself! Then I realized the only Spanish song I know is "Cumbaya," and we weren't even sure if that was really Spanish. Besides, singing would only aggravate my sore throat (catching Megan's cold/swollen glands). Maybe another night.

Right. And maybe another night I'll dress up in a sequined matador suit and fight a bull.

Midway through the evening I put my mirrored sunglasses on because the smoke was irritating my eye again (the rose-tinteds have mysteriously disappeared—probably pickpockets). As soon as I put them on, eighty-year-old singing man turned to Richie and initiated a brief Spanish interchange, presumably:

"Your brother, he is Erik Estrada?"

"No, he is Señor Poos."

I nodded off around two A.M., but I don't think Richie noticed, thanks to my shades. Then Richie's friend Andy came bounding in to meet us and the first thing out of his mouth was, "How come you guys got here so early?" Andy was this hippie kid with wild spirals of red hair, dressed in beat-up army pants and a rugby shirt he described as "old school." Megan asked him where he planned to travel when the semester was done, and he was like, "Wherever, ya know, just cruise around, maybe check out Amsterdam, Prague, anywhere, everywhere . . . keep rollin' till the pesos run out."

What I'd like to know is this: When exactly do you reach the point where you start meeting people who remind you of yourself when you were their age?

And when do you reach the point where you start feeling jealous?

"So how about you birds? Ricardo here tells me this is his last night third-wheelin' it with you two." Andy really talked like that. Birds.

I started telling him how we'll be renting a car tomorrow and heading to the bed-and-breakfast I booked online for our last couple of days alone, and how it's this nine-room estate in the mountains, really isolated and quiet, and how the food is supposed to be phenomenal and the room we requested has a four-poster bed, and then I suddenly started feeling very self-conscious because I suddenly remembered that I was talking to a kid who probably thinks it's fun to sleep on train station steps.

"Okay, dude," I said, trying to recover. "The best part is, it's only a hundred bucks a night. You guys should really check it out."

Andy nearly choked on his clove cigarette. "*Only* a hundred bucks? No offense, hombre, but what have you been drinkin'?"

At this point I had nothing to lose. I said I was reasonably certain it was chamomile tea.

Semester Abroad

This weekend = *IN*tense. Keith, Ingrid, Denise, Sari, Little Joe, me+Megan (♥♥♥♥♥♥) took the ferry to Sweden and it turned out to be the grand opening of the Hard Rock Cafe in Stockholm! It was awesome—not *as* awesome as Hard Rock London but way tastier burgers (and watermelon schnapps) than Hard Rock Paris. I'm sure everyone back at NYU will freak when they see me in the T-shirt because the realization I've had about Americans is that, unlike Swedes, they are all so sheltered. It's like they think the only Hard Rocks are in the United States.

Later on we went to this dance club that was in *Let's Go!* and the DJ was so psyched that we were Americans that he played "Born in the USA" even though we kept requesting Abba since we're in Sweden and we are making an effort not to act like ethnocentrics. The best was when he played "Every Little Thing She Does Is Magic" which was so weird because of how that song *always* reminds me of Megan, and it was so excellent because it felt like it was just me and her out there on the dance floor alone which was so bizarre because it was like the first time I can ever remember that I didn't hate dancing anymore.

Everyone wussed out and went back to the hostel early (approx. 2:20 A.M.), but me+Megan shut the place down and when the bartender finally kicked us out, the *sun* was coming up.

Week Abroad

Best night of sleep we've had all week. This B&B is perfect—out in the middle of nowhere, surrounded by nothing but farms and mountains and sheep. Not a Klansman as far as the *ojo* can see. And the *ojo* CAN indeed see, probably because I wised up and went off my meds yesterday. It finally occurred to me that any remedy calling for chamomile eye-tea and horrible drops that turn your vision orange is obviously some Spanish witch doctor's way of torturing tourists. Megan is sitting on our balcony, writing postcards. Yesterday she scored some Nyquil from the lady who owns the inn. We both dosed ourselves and spent the afternoon culturally immersed in bed (king size, six pillows). When we finally got up, a little while ago, we thought about driving to Malaga (*Frommer's* says there's a good cathedral) or Marbella (*Karen Brown's Guide* says there's a Michelin four-star restaurant) but we opted instead to take a walk in the olive groves behind the inn. Smartest decision we made all week. It's like I was trying to tell Richie when I gave him that farewell talk about the true meaning of travel. If all you want to do is tear through a country hitting every tourist attraction in your path, you may as well go on one of those air-conditioned bus tours, like some kind of old fart.

Confession:

"My social circle has shriveled and shrunk."

Why I Have No Friends

THE INVITATION to my high school reunion got me thinking about certain things, but whether or not to go wasn't one of them. Of course I wouldn't go. It's not that I remember having an especially bad time in high school, or an especially good one, for that matter. All I remember is being very groggy during that particular era. For me, high school was just a way to kill time until embarking on a lifestyle that didn't start so early in the morning.

What the invitation did get me thinking about was my old friends—the ones from high school, but also the ones who came before and after, and proceeded to vanish from the atmosphere somewhere along the way. I'd always thought I was pretty good at keeping in touch, but the facts spoke for themselves. Of the three people I consider my old-est pals, I have not actually talked to one of them for two years, and the other for . . . beats me. As for the third, a guy I've known ever since we both played the part of gums who get attacked by plaque in our fourth-grade production of *Hygiene Heroes,* I am pleased to report that I've kept abreast of his life with the keen interest of a loyal friend. I am not pleased to report that I have done so via my mother, who mails me a steady stream of newspaper clippings about him so I can see how much more successful than me he has be-come.

So how does it happen exactly, this gradual drifting from our oldest of chums? In lieu of attending my high school reunion, I conducted an in-depth analysis of my own personal estrangements. Perhaps my findings will shed light upon yours as well.

20%: Friends Lost to "Coupling Up"

I don't mean coupling up like it was in the halcyon days, when "couple" was defined as the relationship two people shared until putting their clothes back on. I mean grown-up coupling, in which these two people keep these clothes in a shared closet, typically a walk-in that has been remodeled by a certified storage consultant. The grown-up version pre-sents far greater challenges to one's friendships, especially when one cannot stand to be in the same room with the in-sufferably obnoxious/obsessively controlling/stunningly bor-ing mates of one's friends.

Not that I would know.

One thing I do know about couples is that they just require fewer friends than normal people do. And speaking as one of them (someone in a couple, not a normal person), let me tell you why: we get all the social interaction we need from the other member of our couple. For instance, last night, Megan and I sat on the couch and perused the newspaper. Well, that's a social activity right there when you're in a couple. Then, at one point, I got up off the couch to get a drink of water. But before I did, I turned to her and said, "I am getting a drink of water. Would you like one as well?"

"No, thank you," she replied. "But I would like a drink of juice." And then I said, "What kind?" and then she said, "Orange," and before you knew it, we were engaged in a stimulating give-and-take-style dialogue about how the orange juice with calcium tastes a little weird and why would that be.

So you see, we couples participate in a constant whirlwind of sizzling social interaction simply by living under the same roof, which would explain why we might become less inclined to keep up with old friends. It would also explain why some old friends would be less inclined to keep up with us. I am referring specifically to those old friends who have *not* coupled up. I am referring to those eligible, fun-loving, red-blooded bachelors and bachelorettes who would sooner spend the evening sandpapering their skin than hanging out with married people. Especially those who sit on their couch talking about orange juice.

A while ago, I made an effort to see more of the single friends I'd been losing touch with. Once a week, I organized a boys' night out where a few of us would get together to fraternize. They'd fill me in on their latest endeavors, such as the twenty-five-year-old Pilates teacher with the red devil tattoo on her left buttock, and I'd fill them in on mine, such as the window treatments Megan and I chose for the guest room. Maybe it was my imagination, but it always seemed like I was more interested in their lives than they were in mine.

10%: Friends Lost to Procreation

As I further contemplated what happened to my old bosom buddies, it became clear that widespread reproductive activity has forced many of them underground. Generally speaking, the only times I see my friends who've had kids is when I appear at their homesteads bearing pizza. Megan and I did this most recently last Sunday to get reacquainted with our old friends Ben and Erin, currently appearing as Benand-ErinandEliandSammy.

When we arrived, Eli was airborne, having launched himself off the coffee table and around Ben's neck. He then yelled "HI-YA!" while pummeling Daddy about the head and shoulders. He then released his choke hold, resumed his stance on the coffee table, and struck again. And again. And . . .

Conducting a conversation was a little challenging, but I just took my cues from Ben, who was trying to act nonchalant as his offspring attempted to assassinate him. Occasionally, between gasps for air, he'd even try to move the conversation along by following up on something I said earlier. "So, what color are those window treatments again?" he'd say.

Meanwhile, Megan was in the kitchen catching up with ErinandSammy.

Megan: "So, now that we're partnering with another company, I had to ask my assistant to revise the budget report to allot the marketing money we'll need to support the project."

Erin: "You and your brother are going straight to bed unless you take those pepperonis off your eyes *now*."

Don't misunderstand. I am very fond of BenandErinandEliandSammy. I am very worried about adding them to the list of friends I've lost by dint of procreation. And that's why the next time I visit them, I will be bearing something even more thoughtful than pizza. I will be bearing a babysitter.

• • •

The loss of all remaining friends is accounted for below:

10%: MONEY
10%: GEOGRAPHY
50%: TIME

I will now expound upon each factor in descending order, beginning with: **money.** The way I figure it, all my friends were pretty much in the same economic boat when we were first starting out, falling into the tax bracket officially known as "piss-poor." Then some of us stopped being

piss-poor. Some of us even stopped being "cautiously comfortable." Some of us actually became "fabulously well-to-
do." Those of us who wrote this book do not fall into that last
tax bracket, much to our chagrin. This has made it somewhat challenging to socialize with those of them who do.

I'll give you an example of what I'm talking about. Currently, my fabulously well-to-do friend and I get together on
a regular basis of zero to one times per year. Last year, it was
at a party he threw with his fabulously well-to-do wife in
their new home, the pantry of which is bigger than our bedroom, not that I am jealous or anything, especially of those
leather couches—plural—in their *library,* which I've been
coveting ever since I spotted them in the Sundance catalogue for a killionmillion dollars each.

As my fabulously well-to-do hosts served lobster and
poured champagne, I couldn't help but recall that, not too
long ago, I used to meet them at the A&P deli counter on
Saturday afternoons because that was when you'd get the
free string-cheese samples. Now, it felt like we were at some
kind of costume party where we were supposed to come
dressed as sophisticated, affluent adults.

Then I realized something. They *are* sophisticated, affluent adults. No wonder we've drifted apart.

I have also forgone several companions through the
years due to: **geography.** Some of my friends have moved
away so many times, I no longer know where they live. This
has made it difficult to visit them. But if there's a silver lin-
ing to this age when one's peers scatter across the globe, it is
this: it makes you appreciate the rare few with something
truly special to offer. This explains why many successful

long-distance friendships involve someone who has a ski house in Aspen.

Next on my list of friend-losing factors, we have: **time.** Or, at least, we used to have time. Now nobody has it. We don't have time to call our friends like we used to. We don't have time to write our friends like we used to. We *certainly* don't have time to do anything—what's that word again?— *spontaneous*, like we used to.

Typical Interaction When We Still Had Time

Friend One: Hey. What are you doing?

Friend Two: Nothin'. What are you doing?

Friend One: Nothin'. Wanna drive to New Zealand?

Friend Two: Pick me up in five minutes.

Typical Interaction Today

Friend One: Hey. What are you doing Saturday?

Friend Two: Which Saturday?

Friend One: Six Saturdays from next Saturday.

Friend Two: I have an opening at four-thirty A.M.

Friend One: Four twenty-five is better for me. I have to be someplace at four-thirty.

Friend Two: Four twenty-five to four-thirty it is!

Friend One: Perfect. Let's talk next week to reschedule.

But don't you worry, I have reason to believe we're moving into a new phase that could breathe some life into our flailing friendships. I first noticed it a few weekends ago, when Megan was away on business and I spent my stag weekend living it up. On Friday night, I organized all the crap in the basement for the garage sale we've been planning to have for the past ten years. On Saturday night, I enjoyed a bowl of Franco-American Spaghetti and listened to my old albums, which I rescued from the garage-sale pile. But on Sunday night, I busted out. I hit the road and headed to my local video store. I ran into my friend Brian over in Action/Adventure, the first time I'd seen him in months.

"So, you're a bachelor for the weekend!" Brian said. "Why didn't you call me to hang out?"

I told him the truth. I said I didn't call him because I always figure he'll be busy, which he said was ironic since he doesn't call me because he always figures *I'll* be busy, which led me to wonder how many other friends I've lost not as a result of coupling up or procreation, money, geography, or time, but just because we assumed each other's lives had grown far too complicated to accommodate an old friend. Maybe a more accurate scenario is that we're all just wandering around Blockbuster Video, longing to feel part of a group, a crowd, a clique again.

I suppose that's why people go to high school reunions. Myself, I prefer a more personal approach. One by one, I am going to track down each of the cronies I've lost touch with, and I am going to assume that they are all dying to hear from me. First on my list: this kid I grew up with named Petey Ogden. Last I heard, he was renting a ski house in Aspen.

Death of a Sailsman

WHEN COMING ABOUT, head up to a
close-hauled position while pushing
the tiller and steering the bow
through the eye of the wind, and center the rudder when
close-hauled on the new tack."

Debbi, a hale and happy Community Boating instructor dressed from cap to boat shoes in green, meant this tip to
be helpful. And it would have been, if I'd had any idea what
the fuck she was talking about.

It was six P.M., and twenty of us—a fairly pasty bunch
spanning several generations and Teva styles—were gathered on a sunny dock by the Charles River Esplanade. Debbi

was in a small sailboat called a Mercury (or something), teaching us how to rig a jib (I think), which entailed getting the sail up the big metal pole (as far as I could gather).

Occasionally, I'd glance around to see if my classmates seemed equally bewildered by all this talk of luffing, tacking, and gybe ho-ing. They did not. So I continued fake-nodding the way I used to in ninth-grade geometry, before blackmailing my older brother into doing all Venn diagram–related homework for me. The sooner we hit the river, the better, as far as I was concerned. No way was I going to be the remedial rigger who kept the class back with a bunch of dumb questions.

Well, maybe one.

"I might have missed this, but does the centerboard do pretty much the same thing as the starboard?"

Debbi smiled politely, and my classmates had a good chuckle. I think they thought I was kidding.

● ● ●

Before moving to Boston, my seafaring experience consisted mainly of a JetSki ride in Ft. Lauderdale and a Carnival cruise to St. Thomas, which I barely remember because I was tripping on Dramamine at the time. But living in Boston without learning to sail seemed like living in Denver without learning to ski, or living in New York without learning to smoke. I'd been fantasizing about it since I first saw those graceful white sloops from my vantage point on the Red Line trolley. At the time—rush hour—my thought process went something like this:

- Those people are floating tranquilly along the Charles River.

- I am standing in an un-air-conditioned subway next to a lady who's wearing a beekeeper's hat and yelling at a pizza crust on the floor.

- Something must be done to rectify this situation.

As usual, I never did any rectifying beyond sponging invitations off any and all boat-owning individuals who were hard up for some company. I always enjoyed these expeditions. As a professional passenger, sailing allowed me to pursue three of my primary interests: (a) sitting, (b) drinking beer, and (c) letting someone else do the work.

To tell you the truth, I used to take a certain amount of pride in these skills. But lately, my slacker m.o. seems pathetic. It represents a side of myself that's passive, not active; complacent, not adventurous; Gilligan, not Skipper. A side that has always made the excuse that sailing—as opposed to being sailed—is for those who grew up near the Chatham Yacht Club, not the Paramus Park Mall. So after a decade of landlubbing, I made up my mind to become an old salt.

After all, there comes a time in a man's life when he must take his place at the helm, or whatever it's called.

MARINER'S LOG: Introductory On-Water Instruction: The Voyage Begins

6:30 The Charles, she is an enchanting siren who can make even the Red Line trolley look kind of cool here within her waters. I have been aboard the three-man vessel for thirty seconds, since fleeing Debbi's lesson on knots. There were reef knots, granny knots, and an array of advanced-placement knots that looked exactly like the other knots. The only thing these knots have in common is that they are not known as knots. They are known as hitches. Already, I've been enlightened to an essential truth of the sea: for every English word, there is a new and more irritating sailing word.

And so it was that I decided to cut class and skip directly to the sailing part, an option in which Community Boating grads take new students out on the water to show them the ropes. I mean the halyards.

6:40 My crew consists of Anu, the beautiful and able-bodied helmswoman from Bombay; and Trent, an advanced student from Back Bay. Anu's able body is wearing a black hot-pants-and-tank-top ensemble, and I suspect that Trent, a man of few words, has been untying its alluring loops and hitches with his eyes. Moments ago, he broke the ice. "I am in corporate development for Metropolitan Dental Partners," he said. Anu replied that she does portfolio analysis for a private foundation. I sense potential for passion on the high waters.

7:00 "Ready, about," says Anu, and once again, I am nearly beheaded by the boom, a/k/a the thing that is attached to the other thing. I'd been distracted by a lone kayaker paddling into the sunset, who was freed of halyards and cleats and knots known as hitches. For the remainder of the journey, however, I shall assume the seated fetal position to reduce the risk of head wounds.

7:12 I have developed a charley horse from the crouching. Also, rope burn from the one I sat on by mistake.

7:25 We are cruising at approximately no miles per hour when I get up the gumption to take control of the ship. Emerging from the fetal position, I make my way to the bow—no, the stern—where I gingerly take over the tiller—no, the rudder—from Anu. As I do, she tightens her life preserver.

For a moment, I am empowered. When I push the steering thing to the right, the ship turns to the left. When I push to the left, the ship turns to the right. And when the wind suddenly kicks up and sets the ship on a collision course with a Duck Tour Boat, I find myself in violation of Community Boating Rule #18: *Foul language may result in suspension of membership privileges.*

7:26 I demonstrate my mastery of "heeling," which, translated into English, means: "unintentionally tipping the boat on its side for an up-close bacteria analysis/taste-test of the majestic Charles."

7:27 Anu says, "Maybe I'll take over from here." Trent doesn't laugh when I suggest calling the Coast Guard.

7:45 We begin the journey ashore. Resuming the fetal position, I reflect upon what lies ahead: Shore I and II class; Mainsail class; Jib, Spinnaker, and Rhodes 19 class; Sonar, Laser, and High-Performance Sloop I and II seminars.

The voyage from slacker to sailor is longer, harder, and one million times less relaxing than I ever imagined. Yet I shall return to these waters again. And when I do, it will be in a kayak.

Confession:

"I became attached to a major home appliance."

The Day I Turned Unkool

H E STARTED ACTING ill on Monday, but I figured the buzzing noise would go away by itself. The vibrating began on Tuesday, degenerating into violent, shaking seizures later that night. On Wednesday, his breath was labored and warm, and he began to hemorrhage freon. Words were not necessary when Megan and I awoke Thursday morning tangled in sweat-soaked sheets. We just knew. Our treasured friend and air conditioner, known to its admirers as Mr. Kool, had died in our sleep.

He will be profoundly missed.

For some, the loss of an air conditioner is no cause for tears. They believe that heat rash builds character, and a low electric bill is a source of pride. If they get hot, they open a window, or treat themselves to the guilty thrill of an oscillating fan. For them, summer is a time to head for swimming holes and to dine alfresco on melon balls.

When I envision a perfect summer's day, however, I can think of no better place to spend it than in a refreshing, air-conditioned chamber, preferably with drawn shades, a frosty cocktail and/or iced espresso beverage, and a TV tuned to the Cartoon Network, in front of which I will be arranged horizontally.

Place me out of doors on one of those blistering afternoons when the mercury climbs above 60°, and I become foul-tempered and glum. But point me in the direction of an air conditioner, and my will to live soon returns. Air conditioning has that power for me. When I close my windows and shut my door, its hypnotic whir transforms my office into a dominion of worker productivity. And when evening falls, what I like to do best is take a cold shower and stand soaking wet in front of Mr. Kool.

Forgive me, for the pain is still raw. That's what I *liked* to do, before Mr. Kool passed away.

● ● ●

I first bonded with Mr. Kool the summer I turned fifteen. Even then, he was heavy for his age, but with his brown plastic vent and wicked neato air-control lever, to me he was the vision of mod. In slanty letters beneath his Emerson manufacturer's logo read a single word destined to become his namesake: *Kool.* That's how he spelled it, and I admired his go-to-hell spirit. It was the free-wheeling seventies, and my mom, perhaps out of some misplaced guilt about subjecting her children to a broken home, let me decorate my room in her new house however I wanted. The result was Greg Brady–on-mushrooms decor: foil Mylar wallpaper with cork flecks on one wall, driftwood paneling on another, a swirling stucco ceiling, wall-to-wall shag, and a black-and-white Formica bedroom set (with chrome accents) called BunkTrunk. At the center of it all, in a window framed by high-gloss black paint and silver Levolor blinds, sat good old Mr. Kool, his side flaps fanned out with pride.

Those were the wonder years for my air conditioner and me, full of change and discovery. One summer, I was a freckle-faced teen who turned to Mr. Kool after mowing lawns; the next, I was a bloodshot burnout who cranked him up while smoking grass. In August of tenth grade, for reasons still unbeknownst to me, I took up the activity of jogging. The only reward, as far as I recall, was an extended cool-down period, splayed out on my BunkTrunk with Mr. Kool blowing and a pair of giant padded headphones pounding the song stylings of Supertramp into my skull. And on those steamy suburban nights when a young man's mind turned to unpure thoughts of the Cheryl Tiegs poster hanging on his Mylar and cork-flecked wall, let's just say my fantasies were safe with Mr. K.

Mr. Kool and I moved into our first apartment in Somerville (then known as Slummerville), Mass., after I graduated from NYU. My new roommates had convinced me that any object that wasn't obtained from (a) the co-op or (b) the curb was a politically incorrect indulgence—especially if it destroyed the ozone layer. So I held to my principles and did not buy a new air conditioner. Instead, I drove down to my mom's house and absconded with Mr. Kool (and a set of butter knives, but don't tell her). And when I snuck him inside our apartment, you'd best believe I became the toast of the town. My pals put aside their foolish concerns over the greenhouse effect and gathered in my room for a climate-controlled luau, complete with blow-up Splashy Pool from Store 24.

Mr. Kool truly hit his stride when we moved in with my girlfriend, who later became my wife. (I'd like to think you-know-who had a little something to do with that.) On one occasion, we surprised her when she got home from work. It was a stifling July evening and the scent of fried garbage hung in the air outside. Megan stumbled into the bedroom to change into something dry, and—*voilà!*—there she found us: me, seated in my underpants at a milk crate set for two (take-out cold sesame noodles); and Mr. Kool, cheerfully sharing not only his gift of cold air but also his ability to drown out the sounds of the scary coughing man who lived down the hall.

Mr. Kool went through a difficult phase when we finally outgrew him. Well, Megan outgrew him. I have never outgrown anything, which may explain how Mr. Kool wound up in my study along with an eight-track player and a Cheryl Tiegs poster of great sentimental value. Our bedroom became host to a mini Panasonic from Circuit City, and Mr. Kool, by this time a rusty old has-been with missing knobs, brittle side flaps, and a vent held together by Krazy Glue, fell victim to my shameful neglect. I shoved him in the window, stuck bumper stickers on both sides to fill in the gaps, and left him there all winter. He lost his balance during the blizzard of '96 and fractured his air-control lever on the floor. In retrospect, I fear it was a self-inflicted wound. And I will have to live with that for the rest of my life.

On the bright side, Mr. Kool was reunited with us the summer we purchased our first—and, God willing, last—home. In our eagerness to close the deal, we carelessly forgot to ask the realtor, "Does this house conduct heat?" The answer turned out to be yes, and that namby-pamby Panasonic from Circuit City was suddenly in way over its head. Hence, Mr. Kool staged a major comeback in the twilight of his years. All summer long, he performed like a machine half his age. But on Thursday morning, estimated time of death 7:15, he could no longer take the heat.

Today, I mourn the loss of one who touched many lives with the simple gift of conditioning the air. Mr. Kool, my special friend, I haven't been the same since the day you departed.

Maiden Voyage

SOMETHING HAS CHANGED in the Zevin household. Where once there were cartons of aging moo goo gai pan strewn about the living room floor, there now is a carpet clean enough to walk on. Where once there was a strain of bacteria breeding in the bathroom, there now is aquamarine water in the toilet bowl. Where once there was disorder and dirt, there now is Edma.

Edma is our new . . . please bear with me as I search for a p.c. code word to allay the shame. Usually I call her something like "the person who cleans our place every other week for just fifty bucks, the amount you'd drop in a *second* for a few CDs, and I really feel *good* about the fact that she is a South American immigrant who barely speaks a word of English because I believe that in my own small way I am doing my part to help provide for her three school-aged children."

The truth is, I've never thought of myself as someone who's entitled to have a Person Who Cleans Our Place Every Other Week. I don't mean I've never thought of myself as a vile slob—I've been in touch with that self-assessment for a couple of decades now, most recently when the guy at Micro Center said the problem with my computer was that half-and-half had congealed under the L key. It's just that I always thought maids were for fancy middle-aged couples with award-winning offspring and country club memberships and single-family dwellings with more than one bathroom.

But me and Megan? We're just not the kind of couple who have *servants*. We are, however, the kind of couple who have *jobs*—one of which (hers) entails reporting to an actual place of employment every morning, and schlepping home every night without a whole lot of enthusiasm for dusting. As for myself, the stay-at-home scribe, I also have no time to clean the house all day. I'm too busy messing it up.

Here, I'll give you an idea of what I'm talking about. Right now, I am situated in the room I generously refer to as my home office. Every inch of surface space is completely camouflaged by pieces of paper. Unruly wads of scrap paper, yellow squares of Post-it paper, greasy paper plates, crumpled paper towels, notebook paper, printer paper, and ripped-out pages of newspaper that I'm sure are very important because they are paper-clipped to other scraps of paper. (I won't even get into the condition of the floor except to say I think it is one of the dog bones that is making that smell.)

But here's my conflict: I don't feel at home with the severely lived-in look. Sure, it was cool back when I shared a series of dumps with a series of guys even more slovenly than myself. Tim used to stack encrusted bowls of macaroni and cheese next to the ant traps on top of the refrigerator. Peter had a collection of footwear so lethally pungent that your eyes would burn if you entered his room without protective goggles. Back then, anyone who went to the laundromat more than once a month was obviously a clean freak with nothing better to do.

Now that I've matured into an older, more tightly wound individual, I look at my mess and I grow uneasy. It makes me tense; anxious; paralyzed by the fact that I'll never attain that Feng-Shui business I saw in an article I ripped out of one of those magazines I piled on top of the toaster.

But am I anxious now? No, I am not. And that, my friends, is because in exactly two days from today, Edma will return. Wonderful, yellow-bucket-toting, rubber-glove-wearing, sink-scrubbing, mommy-replacing, life-changing Edma (whose three school-aged children I am helping to provide for).

● ● ●

Before Edma, it was not uncommon for Megan and me to spend entire Saturdays engaged in such red-hot couples' action as scouring stubborn grime off our shower tiles. On Sundays, we'd get up early for a quickie—DustBusting, perhaps, or maybe experimenting with something new, like Bon Ami cleanser with phosphates. But soon we grew tired of spending our only time together fighting filth. I grew tired first (surprise, surprise), which caused many painful domestic disputes . . .

> Megan: Why has this pot of dirty water with mold-spore floaters been sitting on the stove for two weeks?
>
> Me: Because it needs to soak. Don't be so fussy.
>
> Megan: *Silence (forty-eight hours).*

We've since worked through those difficult days of our relationship, and we owe it all to the Person Who Cleans Our Place Every Other Week. Let me tell you something about Edma. True, she doesn't have a whole lot to say, but give this woman a bedroom littered with laundry, a kitchen counter stickier than packing tape, and a hallway light fixture coated with bulb-fried bugs, and she will give you a showplace fragrant with lemon-fresh Pine-Sol. Did you know that Edma has a special ceiling-dusting device with a telescoping handle? It is true. I once watched in amazement as she removed what I can only assume was a cobweb invisible to my untrained eye.

I have seen Edma wash the inside of a pencil sharpener. I have witnessed her vacuuming a couch. When she first started, I worried she'd find something personal in her mission to ferret out and clean all known matter in the universe. But now I know Edma does not pass judgment. If she happened upon a pair of his-and-her nipple clamps, she'd just buff them up to a dazzling no-streak shine and place them on the coat rack for all to admire.

In conclusion, I'd like to reiterate that there are still

times I look around my humble abode and feel it's just not right for me to have a Person Who Cleans Our Place Every Other Week.

I mean, there's *definitely* enough crap around here to get her over every other day.

"I sought professional help."

Suddenly Crazy After All These Years

M Y IDEA OF psychotherapy was shaped by too many Saturday nights spent watching *The Bob Newhart Show*. Every week, Bob's crew of zany but lovable patients would be greeted by a wise-cracking receptionist—Carol, I think her name was—and proceed to share their neuroses in a manner that ensured the laughs just kept on comin'. It wasn't until years later that I learned therapy wasn't really for kooky misfits, but for mentally unstable, chemically imbalanced, schizophrenic lunatics like Sally Field in *Sybil*, the made-for-TV miniseries to which I owed this broader understanding. My high school Intro to Psych class taught me that therapy was for nuts with nervous conditions like "trichotillomania," and my college Intro to Psych course taught me that therapy was for—well, now that I think about it, my college Intro to Psych course taught me nothing, since I have no recollection of actually attending it. Every now and then, though, I do recall hearing hushed gossip around the dorm about this stinky weirdo on the fifth floor—this kid who always sat in the hall with his transistor radio—who supposedly went to some mysterious "campus counseling center" that nobody seemed to know the location of. (Or, more likely, nobody admitted to knowing.) Even several years out of school and into my enlightened entry-level life, something made me realize I still stigmatized those who saw a shrink. Flipping through an HMO pamphlet in search of a dentist, I was surprised to come across an entire section devoted to: PSYCHO-THERAPY (*sic*). Seeing the word in print that way only reinforced the way I'd come to define it: therapy, obviously, was for PSYCHOS.

Therapy was not, ergo, for me. What I'm about to say may come as a shock, but, not long ago, I was the guy everyone considered "the normal one." It is true. Ever since I was a teenager, my friends would call me up to unload their problems. I prided myself on my ability to dispense the kind of blunt advice I must have picked up from all those asinine talk-radio shrinks who came on after *Bob Newhart.* "Your girlfriend comes from a dysfunctional family," I'd assert. "Dump her." "Your landlord is in denial. Have an intervention by Wednesday." As the normal one, it was my pleasure to tell them exactly how to solve their problems. If you couldn't turn to your friends during the tough times, who could you turn to?

The answer, I've since ascertained, is that you could turn to a *real* therapist. And at this juncture, nearly everyone I know has. They're not kooky misfits or schizophrenic lunatics, and they're definitely not PSYCHOS, though I do have my suspicions about one (or three) of them in particular. Mostly, they say they went into therapy to be more "self-aware."

Being self-aware is perhaps the one and only thing I myself have never had a problem being. I am so self-aware, you may have noticed, that I have written an entire book about myself. And thanks to my keen self-awareness, nary a word of this book was written without me self-awarely thinking to myself: *What makes you think anyone would want to read an entire book about* you? *The reviewers will call you just another aging gen-X'er so nauseatingly consumed with public navel-gazing that you should just forget about writing and get a webcam instead.*

As if there are going to be reviewers.

As if you could figure out how to use a webcam.

It dawned on me that this kind of thinking was maybe a little *too* self-aware. That maybe it had become self-*conscious,* self-*recriminating,* that, ultimately, maybe it was becoming self-*defeating.*

I didn't tell anyone but my trusty wife, Megan, about my decision to have my head examined, and even made her swear that mum was the word. It didn't matter that all our friends were in therapy, too. That only made it worse. I imagined how betrayed they'd all feel if they found out I wasn't the normal one after all.

> Friend A: Did you hear that *Dan* is seeing a shrink? I can't believe I used to go to *him* for advice when he was just as messed up as the rest of us!
>
> Friend B: I knew I should never have had that intervention with my landlord.

As we see, I wasn't too wild about the idea of anyone analyzing me, a trait that doesn't exactly lend itself to the therapeutic process. On my first few appointments, even the waiting room—a quiet corner painted in earth tones and muted by the calming static of a white-noise machine—aggravated my overactive self-awareness. First of all, there was the possibility of running into someone I knew. But what really stressed me out were the magazines. The waiting room literature consisted of *Us, Poets & Writers, Sports Illustrated,* and *Newsweek.* I wondered if this was some sort of trick—that when my therapist came in to get me and saw which magazine I'd picked, he'd make some kind of analysis based on my choice. I went with *Newsweek.* What could he possibly think about a person who reads *Newsweek*? To me, *Newsweek* has always seemed like a nice, normal magazine that anyone who was crazy certainly would not read. *Poets & Writers,* it goes without saying, was out of the question.

But the thing that triggered my chronic self-awareness the most was the part where you're supposed to talk to the therapist. Part of my glitch here was that anything I said could be *over*-analyzed, which is what happened to a friend of mine who told his therapist that he was a runner, and his therapist said, "What is it you're running away from?" (The answer, it became clear when my friend never again showed up, was the therapist herself.) My other concern was that my shrink might casually repeat my deranged musings to his friends and colleagues, some of whom I might know, and others whom I might not know but who would surely be just as disappointed as the rest of the world to learn I'd taken leave of my faculties.

"I've never actually met him," these strangers would say, "but wasn't he always supposed to be the *normal* one?"

I remembered hearing Howard Stern say he made his psychologist sign a nondisclosure agreement, but I was way too self-aware to bring the idea up with mine. He'd take me for a textbook narcissist with paranoid delusions. Not to mention what he'd think if he found out I listened to Howard Stern.

• • •

I guess what I'm trying to say here is that my ideal kind of therapy was the kind where I wouldn't have to talk to the therapist. My ideal therapist was the kind who'd talk *to me,* who would dispense blunt advice and tell me exactly how to solve all my problems. Dr. L seemed to fit the bill at first— slightly graying around the temples, turtleneck sweater, the kind of high-caliber leather chairs that suggest an individual who knows what's what. But a big talker he was not. What he was, was a big asker. I don't think we were ten minutes into my first session when he started prying into my personal life. You know how a regular just-getting-to-know-you chat usually involves questions like "How are you?" A Dr. L just-getting-to-know-you chat involved questions like "Do you sleep naked?"

For a while, I couldn't help thinking the dude was just nosy. I didn't tell him, of course, because I was too self-aware. I mean, it's not like I didn't realize I was *paying* him to be nosy. And anyway, I knew the real reason I was uncomfortable with all the snooping around. In any given conversation, it's usually *me* who does the asking. At weddings, couples go out of their way to seat me at Satan's Table, the one composed of all the stray oddballs—the groom's JV fencing coach, the spinster aunt, the justice of the peace—because they say I can talk to anyone. I'm quite self-aware of the fact that they mean I can *ask* to anyone. Writing about myself is one thing, but talking about myself is something more vexing entirely. Don't ask me why. It's probably because I am one crazy son of a bitch.

Which may also explain why I developed a nervous habit of asking to Dr. L.

"How's that ankle coming along?" I once asked after noticing he'd been limping. "Did you want to get a drink of water before we start?" I inquired another time for no apparent reason. "So, where are you going on vacation?"

The vacation line of questioning was a real risk, by the way, which is why I fired away with the follow-up question, "Am I allowed to ask?" I'd heard about someone who once asked her therapist where she was going on vacation, and all the therapist said was, "Where do you *want* me to go?"

It turned out that Dr. L was going to St. John, someplace I did want him to go, having been there myself and finding it very pleasant for the most part. I was relieved that he told me, but right afterward, he pointed out that my "caretaking tendencies" were all very nice and everything, but they had a certain "self-diminishing" quality that put everyone else's needs ahead of my own.

On second thought, I'm sure he didn't really say it that way. I'm sure he said it more like this:

"Have you ever thought you might have any caretaking tendencies that have a certain self-diminishing quality which put everyone else's needs ahead of your own?"

Like a mythical Sphinx or the host of *Hollywood Squares,* Dr. L delivered wisdom through questions. But I obviously got his point, because I spent the following months being extremely self-aware of my self-diminishing caretaking tendencies. One time, I was at this stultifying cocktail party, drawing some insufferable drone out of his shell, asking him all about his pulsating career as a systems technician analyst. All of a sudden, I heard Dr. L's voice whispering in the back of my head.

"Dan, you don't really give a shit about this stodgy old gasbag," he was saying.

Oops.

"Dan, do you really give a shit about this stodgy old gasbag?" he was saying. "Or do you think this might be another case where your caretaking tendencies are doing that self-diminishing thing again?"

I promptly ended my interview with the systems technician analyst and headed straight for the onion dip.

Maybe this therapy biz was helping! There I was, out in the world, identifying "patterns," getting in touch with "behaviors." Now if only I could put it to work with Dr. L himself. But every time I set foot back in his office, my caretaking tendencies returned. I suspected, perhaps too self-awarely, that this was because Dr. L was someone I really *did* give a shit about. How could I not? By this point, I'd spent an hour a week for the past six months telling him things I'd never told anyone before (though a sampling of individuals through the years have learned that I sleep naked without ever having to ask), and I didn't even know what kind of car he drove. What was his favorite color? Was he a Celtics fan? Once, I noticed a painting in the waiting room that was signed by a guy with his same last name. I assumed it was his son. I also noticed that Dr. L didn't wear a wedding ring. I assumed he was divorced. But if he was, who got custody of the brilliant tortured artist son?

I considered confronting him with these questions in a very non-self-diminishing manner, when I remembered another story a friend once told me about her therapist. This friend was also curious about what kind of person her shrink was in real life. She found out last summer at the beach, where she spotted her psychiatrist wearing a neon-green thong. The encounter proved to be just a little *too* revealing. "I couldn't take her seriously after that," my friend told me. "It was like discussing the deepest issues of my life with Malibu Barbie."

And so I put aside my curiosity about Dr. L, partly since my interest might be viewed as self-diminishing, but mostly since it might lead down the slippery slope of one day running into him in a little Speedo at the beach. (And that, I assure you, would be a major setback.) Yet after all those months, I was still too awkward to spend an hour just riffing about *me,* and still too self-aware to ignore the odds of Dr. L interpreting my awkwardness as a sign that I was as crazy as a cat in a sweater.

What I really needed, I decided, was some material. Every week, I'd scribble some talking points down on a scrap of paper, each good for ten, fifteen minutes. A typical scrap would go something like this: "fight w/Megan; bounced check; sea monster dream (discuss mother/rope)." I'd glance at this outline in the waiting room, between articles in *Newsweek,* but wouldn't dare pull it out during an actual session. The last thing I needed was for Dr. L to discover I was the kind of crackpot who needed a script to talk to his shrink. I was hoping he'd just respond to the material, to feel that, finally, we were getting somewhere. But he never seemed particularly riveted. Take the sea monster dream, for instance. By the time I got to the part about how I was attached to the sea monster by a rope and how the sea monster was pulling me deeper and deeper under water, and then how the sea monster was actually my mother, I was thinking, *This one he's gonna love! This one is gonna give him a chance to say something about the rope symbolizing an umbilical cord or something, and about how that must mean something totally twisted about me and my mother. This one is gonna make him feel useful, like he helped me!*

This urge to make Dr. L feel needed wasn't anything new. A long time ago when I was telling him how I hated to dance unless I was hammered, he asked if I thought taking tango lessons might help. "That's a really good idea," I responded, not wanting to hurt his feelings but knowing that the chances of me ever taking tango lessons were about as good as the chances of me ever tuning in to C-SPAN.

It was even worse with the sea monster dream. No matter how many opportunities I gave him to chime in with some insightful analysis, he appeared thoroughly unimpressed with my material, even the parts that were slightly embellished for dramatic effect. The only thing he responded to was the last, most boring thing that came out of my mouth—something like, ". . . and then I woke up and my wife, Megan, goes, 'it's only a dream.' "

"Why do you think you have to remind me after all these months that Megan is your wife?" he asked.

Inside, I knew exactly why I was reminding him. If this guy was anything like Bob Newhart, he was seeing seven, maybe eight maniacs in addition to myself per day. How could he possibly keep our disorders distinct? I was reminding him not only to help him keep abreast of who had which pathology, but also to help him stay focused on mine, just in case he might have felt himself drifting off and thinking about what he needed to pack for his upcoming trip to St. John (hopefully not a Speedo). I was reminding him because, I don't know about you, but in the Zevin family, if you're talking for more than three minutes without anyone interrupting you, it can mean only one thing: no one is paying attention.

"Huh? Did I just say 'my wife, Megan'? It's nothing, really. It's just the way I refer to stuff—my wife, Megan; my dad, Ronald; my mom . . . the Loch Ness Monster."

He smiled. Didn't crack up or anything, but still. At least he was paying attention.

• • •

I wish I could tell you that on the day I showed up with no material, it was because I was becoming normal again. Alas, it was because nothing really happened that week. So I said something predictable like "I don't have anything to talk about," and he said something predictable like "Why do you need something prepared to talk about?" and who knows why, but ten minutes later I was off on some random tangent about how when I was a little kid, my brother and sister and I used to put on these funny little skits for my parents that we memorized from the *Zoom* activity book, and then for some reason that reminded me of how whenever my parents had company over, I inevitably found myself doing a little magic show for everyone, or demonstrating a little experiment from my chemistry kit, and then *that* total non sequitur led into the whole trampoline thing, the whole seat-drop/swivel-hips/backflip-into-a-front-drop routine I subjected them to anytime they made the mistake of venturing out of doors and into the backyard, where sat the trampoline they gave us as a very elaborate Chanukah present one year.

I was just yapping away, just lettin' it flow, unaware of how any of this was connected, and, even stranger, not terribly concerned that I was coming off as one of those unhinged wackos who walk down the street pushing a shopping cart and discussing topics with themselves that move seamlessly from the impending apocalypse to the Ziploc Bag conspiracy. And on the ride back home from this particular session, I had my first Duh moment.

A Duh moment is the opposite of one of those Aha! moments the asinine talk-radio shrinks were always hyping. Instead of realizing something earth-shatteringly new, you realize something so obvious, so unremarkable, so tell-me-something-I-don't-already-know-about-myself, you wonder how you missed it all this time. For example: "Duh. Maybe the reason certain people are hyper-self-aware is because they spent their childhood calling attention to themselves." Or: "Duh. Maybe the reason certain people spent their childhood drawing attention to themselves was because they were trying to get their parents' attention." Or even: "Duh. Maybe certain people confused getting their parents' attention with getting their parents' approval, and maybe they confused getting their approval with getting everyone else's approval, and maybe *that*—Duh—is why certain people develop certain 'caretaking tendencies' that have a certain 'self-diminishing' quality that puts everyone else's needs ahead of their own."

DUH.

Not to get all healy-feely on you or anything, but I believe that is what they call a "breakthrough" in the therapy game. For one thing, it shed some light on a behavior I'm now working through (you never work "on" anything in therapy, only "through" it), so don't expect a whole lot of caretaking from me anytime soon. Mainly, though, it gave me the confidence to know I didn't really need Dr. L to dispense blunt advice and tell me exactly how to solve all my problems. As long as he kept asking away, I could figure all this shit out on my own.

Which is why I would like to wrap up with a session we

had very recently. I was in the middle of one of my aimless soliloquies about—who knows, it's not like I had a script or something—when I glanced down and noticed the sole of my sneaker was coming apart.

"Jeez, it looks like the sole of my sneaker is coming apart," I remarked.

Dr. L looked at me in that familiar, quizzical way that suggested he was about to ask why I thought it looked like the sole of my shoe was coming apart. But instead, he took a deep breath and made the following pronouncement:

"You should get Shoe Goo for that. It really works."

For the first time in nearly a year, Dr. L had dispensed blunt advice and told me exactly how to solve a problem. Now I just wonder when he's going to notice that I took his advice. I sat with my legs rigidly crossed a few weeks ago, figuring he'd get a better look at the sneaker. My body language probably demonstrated that I was inhibited, or self-conscious, or that I had a long way to go before reclaiming my status as the normal one. At the time, though, none of that stuff even occurred to me.

Call me crazy, but I'm pretty sure that's progress.

My Sweatpants/My Self

DO YOU THINK it's time to lose the sweatpants, maybe?" The words, they stung. Here I was at breakfast, enjoying my Cocoa Puffs, absorbed in *Zippy*, resplendent in my Sunday best. Out of nowhere came Megan's inflammatory remark.

"What, you don't like the sweatpants?" I asked.

"Dan, go look at yourself," she said.

So I did. And as I stood there, staring at my reflection, here is what I saw: an individual in his thirties wearing sweatpants he got at the campus store during Freshman Orientation. Granted, they were a little tighter around the . . . everywhere than they used to be. And, yeah, the peeling decal on the left leg now said N^{V}U instead of NYU. But

123

these nuances represented sixteen years of loyal experience. When I looked those sweatpants straight in the ^{v}, I saw sweatpants with character, sweatpants with history, sweatpants that once found their way into the red plastic laundry basket of Hattie—also known as Hottie—McDonough, if you catch my meaning.

Hell if I was going to abandon them now.

● ● ●

But that, perhaps, is because I've developed a sick attachment to my old clothes. When we moved from our apartment to our house, Megan filled eight (8) Hefty Bags with her old clothes for the Goodwill truckers to haul away. I filled a Dunkin' Donuts bag with a pair of tube socks. (The only reason I tossed the socks, between you and me, is because they had holes in the big toe.)

An impromptu excavation of my wardrobe reveals many fascinating artifacts. In drawer number one lies my first-ever concert jersey (Jackson Browne, Garden State Arts Center, '79). "Wear *me*!" it beckons each morning. "I will make you feel all free-and-easy again!" On the shelf in my bureau resides the unwieldy wool sweater I got in Copenhagen my junior year abroad. "Skøl!" it drunkenly shouts. "I will add a touch of international intrigue to your image!" And who is that hanging in the downstairs closet? Why, it is my old friend the Guatemalan hooded pullover thing I got at the Hemp 'n More Store that summer I drove to Boulder with my former friend Tim! "*Dude,*" it whispers, "slip me on over that twelve-year-old tie-dye in your dresser and you'll be feelin' no pain in no time."

● ● ● ●

Part of my peculiar style of dress stems from my peculiar style of career. As a professional shut-in, or "self-employed person," I am exempt from all dress codes. But I'm starting to think the other part has less to do with my job than my gender. Like many members of the male ilk, I am unable to construct a reasonable "outfit." Well, maybe not so much unable as unwilling. Left to my own devices, I get dressed with one goal in mind: Maximum Comfort. If someone told me that it is extraordinarily comfortable to wear underpants on your head, you'd best believe I'd be sitting here bedecked in a Jockey Shorts bonnet.

Nature or nurture? Who among us can say, really? But according to one public-opinion survey (four friends I e-mailed an hour ago, one of whom still hasn't responded), it appears that the ability to dress oneself in a contemporary manner is consistent with what experts call "blatant gender stereotyping." Women are better at evaluating the way garments relate to each other. Women are more comfortable using verbs like "accessorize." Women can evolve; adapt; wake up one morning in the late 1970s, look in their closets, and scream, "*Gauchos?!* What was I *thinking?!*"

The male fashion sense, particularly amongst the hopelessly hetero, appears to start and end at age fifteen. At least, it did for me:

The year is 1978. The scene is Bobbie's Boys, a clothing store in the Millburn Mall. A glum-looking teenage boy is scouring through the "Groovy Getups" aisle for apparel that is considered haute couture at Millburn Junior High: Levis pre-

125

washed corduroys (straight-legged, not flared) and Timberland boots (beige, unlaced). His mother is at the opposite end of the store in a department called "Dressy Duds."

> Mother: (holding up Andy Gibb–ish velour Jordache dress slacks) "Hey, Daniel! How about these?"
>
> Son: (under his breath) "Yeah, I'll wear those and get my ass kicked from algebra class to the emergency room."
>
> Mother: (holding up a pair of Frye boots similar to those worn by Bo in *The Dukes of Hazzard*) "Hey, Daniel! These boots would look sharp on you!"
>
> Son: "I'd rather wear underpants on my head."

But that was then. Now I just avoid clothes shopping altogether. And on those rare occasions when I do find myself in an establishment where attire is purveyed, I am accompanied not by my mother but by my wife. Megan, you see, feels it is enjoyable to shop. When she sees a garment hanging on a rack, she notices the fabric, the lines, the cut. I notice the little white tag that says it costs $89.99. Then I put it back on the rack and wander over to the clearance section. It's not that I'm cheap, it's that I don't understand the *concept* of spending that kind of money on clothes. I'd rather spend it on travel; entertainment; an *experience*—an experience to which I will wear a flannel shirt from 1978.

● ● ●

Shortly after the sweatpants incident, I received (and more significantly, did not recycle) my weekly delivery of

three identical J. Crew catalogues. What came over me I
don't know, but I wound up buying more new clothes in five
minutes than I had in five years. It wasn't until they arrived
that I realized my new purchases were just updated remakes
of all the old standards. Flannel shirts with goofy zippers instead of buttons. Black (not beige) Timberland ripoffs. A
bad-ass gray down jacket that bears remarkable resemblance
to the green one I used to wear to Millburn Junior High.

Ask me to part with any of these upstarts and I'll have
the Goodwill truck over here pronto. But ask me to lose my
ill-fitting, stained N^{v}U sweatpants from Freshman Orientation, and you're asking me to lose a part of myself.

Make no mistake: when it comes to clothes, I care. I
care enough to wear.

Confession:

"I went to a wine tasting."

. . . .

Cork Dork

ERE'S WHAT I thought when my friend Peter came over with a bottle of wine and said, "I *really* think you'll like it": *What about it does he really think I'll like?* Was it the groovy label? Did it cost eight dollars or less at Thrifty Discount Beverage? Or was it just that it had been sitting around his kitchen ever since someone gave it to him, and he was psyched to finally unload it on someone else?

These, after all, were the most important qualities that *I* looked for when judging any given vintage.

I don't know what's wrong with me, but I still do not appreciate fine wine. I only appreciate fine beer. Okay, that's not quite true. I also appreciate sucky beer. It's not like I'm one of those meatheads who makes windowsill pyramids out of Meister Brau cans (anymore), it's just that I'm sick of being the only member of my peer group who shows up at parties bearing six bottles with caps instead of one with a cork. When I see a wine list at a restaurant, I ignore it, opting instead for a reliable old classic called House Red, if I am having red food, or a splendid little selection known as House White, if I am having white or off-white food. Also, I saw a magazine the other day called *WineX,* a four-color affair aimed at aging X'ers no longer into playing quarters. To me, it was yet another indication that I am developmentally delayed.

Which is why it came to pass that I decided to attend a free wine tasting at the Brookline Liquor Mart last Saturday afternoon. The way I saw it, the first step to becoming a mature adult who appreciates wine was finding out what I was supposed to be appreciating.

●　●　●

Upon arriving at BLM, the first thing I appreciate is that it doesn't cater to the kind of bow-tied blowhards I always assumed went to wine tastings. It's just your average, no-nonsense liquor store, gussied up with a gourmet shop and a row of warm wooden wine shelves. Next to Juice 'N Soda, I spot an extremely random demographic sampling of maybe a dozen people—a Billy Idol–looking dude with a bike messenger bag, a couple in matching Rockports who remind me of my parents' friends the Weisblatts—all milling around a long white table set with eight bottles and some high-rent cheese. Several smiling staffers in BLM polo shirts stand behind the table like bartenders, pouring wine into plastic urine specimen cups.

"Today's theme is 1997 Burgundies," says Lance, a wholesome-looking server who would definitely get carded if he wasn't the one in charge. He hands me a pamphlet describing the various selections, which range from $15 to $60 and are to be tasted in order of white to red, light to heavy. The idea, he explains, is to learn to distinguish between different kinds of wine the same way you distinguish between different kinds of music or art. All you have to do is remember the five S's: see, sniff, swirl, sip, and spit.

"Spit?" I say, shocked that a budding connoisseur such as myself would ever be advised to hack up a mouthful of sixty-dollar wine. It seemed like test-driving a Porsche by revving it up in neutral.

"Spit," says Lance. "Otherwise, all you'll get out of this experience is drunk." He shows me a bucketful of backwash where a gray-haired gentleman is drooling out an exceptionally pungent Macon-Vire.

Clearly, this Lance has been throwing back a few too many Burgundies if he thinks I'm going anywhere near *that* pail of swill.

● ● ●

Our first selection is a Maison Labouré-Roi, Nuits-St.-Georges Montagny, a vintage that makes me glad there's no S for "say." Instead, I set forth to "see," jotting down the following observation about the wine's appearance: "?" The reason the wine appears to be "?" is that I'm observing it through a plastic urine specimen cup. This leaves me no other choice than to skip directly to S number five: swallow (the S formerly known as spit). I practice this S several times with several wines, just to get it right. Soon I'm no longer too self-conscious to take my pamphlet up on its offer to "*Please ask us questions!*"

"So how come those ladies in the warm-up suits over there get *real* wine glasses?" I ask Lance. He says the regulars know the deal is BYOG. But not to worry. Lance disappears into the stock room for a moment, just enough time for me to cleanse my palate with a Gorgonzola sandwich and a Bourgogne urine sampler. Much to my delight, he returns with a generously proportioned glass indeed. I am now equipped to tackle the sniff, which entails evaluating the wine's bouquet, or "nose."

I need to bring up here that my own personal nose could be evaluated—tactfully—as "prominent." So keen are my nasal sensors that I have described certain women as smelling like *Vanity Fair* magazine, and yellow chicken curry as smelling like a locker room. "It smells like Scotch tape in here" is not an unusual thing for me to say.

But when I take a whiff of the Volnay Caillerets, the best I can do is: "Smells like wine." To which the hippie chick next to me says: "Actually, I'm getting oak." Then Mr. Weisblatt. "Leathery," he remarks. "I'm getting pickles," notes his wife. "Yes, pickles," interjects someone else. "And cement."

At this point, I'm certain that these people are screwing with my head. But Lance insists that being "inventive" is one of the goals of describing wine. Here are some descriptions he shares from a diagram called the Aroma Wheel: Kerosene. Cabbage. Wet Dog.

To tell you the truth, I kind of like the smell of my dog

when she's wet. But that doesn't mean I want to make her into a spritzer.

    ● ● ●

By the time we get to the eighth and final wine of the day, I would inventively describe myself as "publicly intoxicated." I have mastered the swirl (in which one shakes one's glass around and says "nice legs, very viscous"). I have modified my sip (in which one takes a *small* amount into one's mouth and whistles backwards to enhance the flavor, or something). I have dropped a glass of sixty-dollar wine that shatters to bits on the floor (upon which one is informed by management that it's now officially Last Call).

But not before one final S: the soft sell. "Can we interest you in any of these wines or anything else in the store?" asks Lance.

I tell him that my friend Sari is having her birthday party later tonight, and there's no way I'm showing up with a six-pack of Pabst. He gets me a bottle of Salvalai Pinot Grigio, which he describes as "friendly" and "grapefruity." I study the bottle and make a few observations of my own. "Groovy label; $4.95."

Several hours and one pot of coffee later, I present Sari with her gift. "I *really* think you'll like it," I say.

Confession:

"I'm no fun anymore."

Don't Play Games

LET ME BEGIN by coming clean to my friends Nicole and Michael: The reason I couldn't make it to your dinner party wasn't really because I was sick. In fact, I experienced a surge of vim and vitality when you first called, just as I always do when presented with the prospect of free food. The threat that followed your invitation, however, caused a wave of dread to pass through me: *After dinner, we are going to play Celebrity.*

"Celebrity," for those of you who have never been forced to play, is a game in which you have to make your partner guess the name of a famous person you pick out of a hat. I, for one, do not care for Celebrity. I also do not care for:

1. Monopoly
2. Trivial Pursuit
3. cards

That was the short list. The long list is: games as a whole. When it comes to games, I'm not what you would call a Player.

Please don't hate me because I don't like games. Please don't get all defensive and belligerent and insistent that I come down from my ivory tower and face up to all the fun I've been missing out on. I assure all you Players out there that I have nothing against any of you. Some of my best friends are Players. I just told you about Nicole and Michael, didn't I? Frankly, the reason I faked sick instead of telling them the truth is because you Players always give me a little attitude, a little tone of voice, whenever I politely decline your offer of games.

"Oh, so Zevin's too *cool* to play games, is that it?" you say to yourselves. "Well, *screw him* if he thinks we're a bunch of goofy, game-playing geeks. I bet the real reason he won't play Parcheesi with us is that he *doesn't know how.*"

You win. I *don't* know how. Seriously. I don't know how to play chess, backgammon, or Balderdash, either. And as for you, Tyler, the reason I never e-mailed you back about "poker night" is that I don't even know how to play *that*. People have tried to teach me for years. But trying to teach me how to play poker is like trying to teach a kangaroo how to do fractions (or like trying to teach *me* how to do fractions, for that matter).

I hate games because they make me feel stupid; inadequate; self-conscious. Do I sound like the kind of partner who's going to lead you to the sweet taste of victory in an after-dinner Celebrity tournament? I'd let you down in seconds, and then you'd hate me even more. The pressure—oh, the pressure.

Sometimes, in my quietest, most melancholy moments, I feel the world is divided into two types of people: people who like the games, and . . . me.

And sometimes, I become bitter. Let me tell you Players something: I used to *like* Celebrity, until I was subjected to my first death match with a group of cutthroat competitors from Cambridge. Oh, excuse *me,* Sean from Harvard Class of '91, for not realizing that Abdullah Ocalan, the Kurdish separatist leader, was a "celebrity." Maybe if you just shot me another dirty look and rolled your eyes a little more to show everyone how dumb I was, I would have gotten it sooner.

And how about you, smartypants Scott, University of Pennsylvania Class of '86? Remember that night we played Trivial Pursuit and your former friend Dan wasn't sure—he actually *did not know*—how many settlers sailed from England on the *Mayflower* in 1620?* Say, what ever happened to Dan, anyway? I'll tell you what happened to him: You dropped him like a hot potato after his unfortunate little Trivial Pursuit performance. You lost all respect for him. You realized he wasn't a Player.

I have witnessed relationships destroyed and ugliness exposed by dint of the games. I have watched my old chum Jim mutate into a bald-faced liar during a round of Scrabble in which he insisted that "tvet" was a word. I have heard sweet, soft-spoken Sharon, a woman who often uses the word "lovely"

*A hundred.

in casual conversation, tell her boyfriend to "piss off!" in a high-stakes Crazy Eights competition. But worst of all, I have felt myself fall prey to the unspeakable evil the games bring about.

It happened with Pictionary in the fall of 1997. My partner was Susan. Her clue was Cleopatra. Her drawing of Cleopatra looked like this:

When I saw that picture, I broke out laughing, grabbed it out of her hand, and held it up for everyone else to laugh at. I hung Cleopatra on my refrigerator when I got home, a memento of the night I actually enjoyed playing a game. A memento of the night I made fun of someone worse at it than me. A memento of the night I finally knew what it felt like to be a Player.

I've never been able to look at Susan the same way again.

• • •

My issues around the games can be traced to an early childhood trauma involving Operation, the do-it-yourself surgery and electrocution game that entailed using a tweezers to remove the organs of a pre-assembled patient. The fun part was that the body was surrounded by an invisible electric fence. Excitedly, I set forth to remove a pancreas, and *bzzzzzzzzz*. Shocked like a Pavlov dog into a game-phobic five-year-old.

As you might imagine, I wasn't the kind of kid who showed a lot of enthusiasm for birthday parties. They all started out safely enough—a little cake, a little clown—but inevitably, some sick PTA mother would strap a blindfold across my face, spin me around, and demand that I stumble across her rec room with a sharp thumbtack in my fist, all in a fruitless effort to pin the tail on the motherfucking donkey.

I had a brief flirtation with games in college, but that's because every game was a drinking game in college. Back then, you could put a Pop-o-Matic in front of me and I'd just pop and pop and pop.

But now I say, "Games? Not for me." I don't even like the games you're supposed to play by yourself, such as solitaire or SimCity or that colored Ruby's Cube thing from a hundred years ago. What the hell were you supposed to do with that thing, anyway? Turn it? Oh, *that's* fun. Almost as fun as crossword puzzles—exactly one of which I have ever managed to complete (*TV Guide*, 4/15/79, Weezie Jefferson on cover).

There is one final game I have been avoiding thus far, as its mere mention causes a terrifying constriction in my trachea. Suffice it to say that if ever you wish to share the name of a movie, book, or person with me, there is no need to yank your ear or point to your nose.

Just cut the crap, tell me what it is, and we can talk about it like adults are supposed to.

My Brush with Detox

YESTERDAY I HAD a headache that suggested a freight locomotive had slammed
through my cranium. But there was some-
thing more mature, more evolved about this particular hang-
over. It came from drinking too little, not too much. I ran out
of coffee. And now, I was suffering the crippling symptoms
of withdrawal.

It was only upon hitting bottom that I could finally face
a decade of denial. My habit was just three mugs a day: one
in the morning, one with—okay, *for*—lunch, and one reserve
cup for whatever glittering activities the evening might
bring, such as *Larry King Live*. I didn't even have one of

those insulated plastic mugs you see your hard-core users toting around town with trembling hands. No. I've always regarded my coffee as though it came with an Rx from the pharmacist: *To increase productivity, administer one cup before turning on computer; to prevent drowsiness during warm-up band, dispense auxiliary mug 10 minutes prior to show time.* I controlled coffee, not the other way around. Or so I thought until my skull-crushing caffeine withdrawal made me realize I had a bona fide chemical dependency. Granted, I laced my chemical with half-and-half, but confirmed control freaks such as myself can't stand being dependent on *anything.* Clearly, it was time to get off the brown stuff.

I viewed my decision not only as a way to get clean, not only as a small gesture of empowerment, but also as an excuse to pay a visit to Mr. Yefim Shubentsov of Brookline, Massachusetts. I'd heard Courteney Cox raving about him on the Jay Leno show. According to Courteney, whom I had no reason not to trust, he was a mysterious healer who cured her nicotine habit. A-list addicts from Billy Joel to Amy Tan have sworn by "the Mad Russian" and his "bio-energy," ostensibly an internal healing force he uses to erase problems ranging from alcoholism to tennis elbow. Actually, I'd been hearing about the guy for years. Everyone seemed to have a friend of a friend whose plumber's brother-in-law ("He smoked thirty-four cartons a *day*—") was cured by the Mad Russian. Could he do anything for my personal addiction? For sixty-five bucks—roughly the price I'd pay on the street for six pounds of primo French roast—I was about to find out.

• • •

"There is nothing *mej-i-kal* here. What I do is *feeesical*, not *sick-o-logical*." The first thing that strikes me about Yefim (besides that he looks like Mel Brooks on creatine) is that his accent is extremely challenging—and not only for the guy in the corner who came for help with a hearing impairment. As Yefim darts around the plush Oriental rug of his warm, denlike office, the eighteen of us seated in a circle are encouraged to discuss our issues. *"Does anybody in thees room hef any pain?!"* he suddenly barks, his disposition shifting from cuddly to creepy. A woman from Chicago answers that, yes, she has ankle pain. Yefim directs a *shazam*-like wave of his hands in her direction. She says her pain is gone. A guy in a flannel shirt says he has neck pain. Yefim punches the air like those televangelists who cure the crippled with a swift smack to the forehead. No more neck pain. When my turn rolls around, I'm fairly certain the shtick is a setup, but I find myself wanting to believe.

> Yefim: *Do you hef any pain!*
>
> Me: Um, I get these wicked caffeine headaches if I
>   don't drink coffee.
>
> Yefim: *If you sit on a nail, you must not take Tylenol.*
>   *You must remove the dem nail!*

Whether or not he had the powers to remove the dem nail remained to be seen, but as Yefim spent the following forty minutes lecturing on topics from Prozac to calisthenics (I think—his accent was hard to understand), I developed an overwhelming urge for something that *could* remove my dem headaches: a delicious, hot cup of coffee.

• • •

One of the things I like best about coffee is that it provides a ritual. Each morning, I open my freezer and remove the Tupperware container that stores my stash. I then secure one of the #4 filters that I have cleverly stored *in* the freezer, right *next* to the coffee, and pack my auto-drip with two (to ten) tablespoons of coffee and three cups of water. When it comes to coffee, precision is everything, especially when you start buying in bags instead of cans.

"Do you hear what I em say-ink!" The Mad Russian is now standing in the corner, facing a wall. For the past five minutes, he has rested his bio-energetic hands over the ears of Hard-of-Hearing Guy. To measure the results, he whispers into the wall: "Seven, seven, seven." Then he asks the guy, clear across the room, what he heard.

" 'Seven, seven, seven'?" says Hard-of-Hearing.

"You see! I am like an eraser!" Yefim boasts. I think.

• • •

Perhaps my most cherished coffee moments have occurred close to home, at the Someday Café. I was a regular there when it was just a hallway next to the Somerville Theater. It's larger now, but still has that comforting feel of an entry-level living room decorated with curbside furnishings. Through the years, I've made many coffee friends at the Someday. We chat, attempt to remember each other's names (both easier after half a cup), then go back to our coffee-supplemented activities: reading the paper; doing our bills; sipping a cup of Costa Rican and staring hopefully through a picture window that's stenciled with the word "Someday."

• • •

"*Who is it?*" Yefim is holding the pottery bust of a historical figure he has removed from his bookshelf. Each of us takes a stab at its identity as we pass it around our circle, a highbrow game of hot potato. "Picasso?" ventures Highway Phobic. "Da Vinci?" posits Chain Smoker. "Beethoven?" guess I, mainly because it seems to me that the majority of bookshelf busts are of Beethoven.

"You are all wrong!" Yefim says (I think). "But that is not the point." I brace myself for some past-life yarn about Yefim erasing Leonardo's glue-sniffing issue. "The *point* is that as long as you are thinking about something else, you are not thinking about your cravings."

• • •

At this juncture, what I'm really thinking about is how suffocatingly hot this room has become, which in turn triggers visions of iced coffee. I always take mine with plenty of cream and sugar, the goal being to make it taste like dessert. One summer, I was in St. Louis visiting my sister and I asked the waitress if they had iced coffee. "I guess," she replied, and proceeded to pour hot coffee into a glass of ice. I have not been back to St. Louis.

At the end of our hour-long motivational magic show, we're each granted one private minute with the Mad Russian, who by this point has expended so much bio-energy that he has actually broken a sweat. I close my eyes, he makes a special wheezing noise that suggests he's got a touch of smoker's cough himself, then it's *ka-ching-ching-ching* off to the cashier. Twenty minutes later, I'm sucking down a French roast at the Someday Café, pleased that I've come up with a more prudent strategy for dealing with my addiction: an insulated plastic mug.

Confession:

"I enjoy getting back to nature."

Boyz in the Woods

IT WAS A refreshing change of pace to wake up in the woods with the smell of Meister Brau and cigars on my breath. Lying beside me was my younger brother, Richie, and lying beside Richie was my surrogate daughter, Chloe. To the outside world it might have looked like we spent the night in some kind of sicko ménage à trois, but the outside world could not see us. We were in a tent—the treasured "U.S. Camper" I scored at a garage sale for $6.50. And as I removed my dog from my forehead and bounded out of my sleeping bag, I was one happy U.S. camper myself.

My city-slicking friends think I'm mental when I tell them I've gotten into camping. They worry about fire ants, poison oak, jackals. They conjure up images of hunting for food with bows and arrows. "Dan," they say to me, "why would a sensible indoorsman such as yourself possibly be interested in roughing it?"

And I say to them, *"Roughing it?"* Roughing it is staring at a computer all day until you've lost your blink reflex; or suffering a near hand amputation in the doors of an SRO subway; or greeting each evening with barely enough energy to nuke the Trader Joe's Stir Fry Shrimp bag that has been fossilizing in your freezer since October. Roughing it is facing the daily quest to be doing, getting, being *more*. Roughing it is all about acting your age.

Camping, conversely, is all about acting my brother Richie's age (nineteen), or, if you're really doing it right, acting my dog, Chloe's, age (three). I'm talking playing in the dirt. I'm talking eating with your hands. I'm talking the simple, sublime act of outdoor urination.

I am living proof that trapped within every indoorsperson, there is an outdoorsperson waiting to be released. And that is why I present you now with some words of advice to make *your* brush with nature a more enjoyable one.

Camping for Reluctant Grown-ups

I. What to Bring Camping

The most important piece of equipment you'll need is a car. This equipment allows you to pull up to—rather than death-march into—your campsite.

Some people (and by "people," I'm referring here to my friend Doug) dismiss this approach as "car camping." Personally, I feel this term is misleading, because it makes it sound like you spend the night in your car, which I have also done, but only once during a flash flood in Maine when I found out why the U.S. Camper cost only $6.50. This brings to light one of my primary tips for the beginning camper: don't pinch pennies when it comes to the optional "rain fly" accessory.

Also, don't go camping with Doug.

Doug is one of your old-school campers who has one of those back-brace-style backpacks with the metal frame on the *outside* (and the inventory of an army-and-navy store on the inside). Doug thinks it is fun to go "winter camping." Doug has many special water filters and tablets that would allow him to quench his thirst with acid rain, but I doubt he'd use them even if he had to. "Giardia?" Doug would scoff, filling his canteen from a cesspool. "Malarkey!"

The reason I'm convinced of this is because once, in a stellar display of poor decision-making, I agreed to accompany Doug on one of his Outward Bound–brand expeditions. I owe the fact that I am writing these words now to his official Red Cross First Aid Kit.

II. Where to Go Camping

A campground should never be mistaken for a playground. Avoid those containing:

- Wet-n-Wild water flumes
- pre-assembled tents shaped like tepees
- any reference whatsoever to Barney Rubble

Remember, the idea is to *act* like a child, not actually come into contact with one.

So, where *should* you go camping? You should go to the place I went with Richie and Chloe. And let me just say that you are high on drugs if you think I'm about to divulge the name of this place. Word gets out, they put up a water flume, and the next thing you know it's Yabba-dabba-doo-land.

III. What to Do When Camping

I heartily recommend the taking of a hike, since it provides us amateur outdoorspeople with a simple, attainable goal. The goal is to get through the hike without dying.

To that end, it's always a good idea to read trail guides before you go, and an even better idea to use them as kindling when (and if) you return. Richie, Chloe, and I learned this lesson together.

What the trail description said: "This relatively easy hike features a steady incline leading to a panoramic view of the White Mountains. (Approx. 3 hrs.)"

What the trail description should have said: "This relatively easy hike—relative to Mt. Kilimanjaro—features an impenetrable, ninety-degree incline before you die. Even your friend Doug, with his Red Cross First Aid Kit, would die on this hike. (Approx. ∞ hrs.)"

Lucky for us, we did not die. Instead, we entered the hiking zone. The hiking zone is when you block out everything but the sound of your own two feet (or four paws) and your mind becomes filled with insight and clarity. It was during just such a moment that I realized my little brother, Richie, wasn't so little anymore, that he had matured into a very wise and thoughtful young Zevin. It happened when he turned to me after two hours and remarked,

"Dude, this sucks. Let's go back and rent a canoe."

IV. What to Eat When Camping

Some people (and by "people," I'm referring to my wife, Megan, and her friends Lucia, Erin, Belinda, and Diane, who celebrated Erin's engagement by going—their words—"girl-camping") enjoy barbecuing elaborate kabobs and making fancy coffee drinks with the REI portable espresso machine they gave Erin as an engagement gift. I, however, believe that campfire cooking—like camping—should be child's play. Here's the dinner menu Richie and I planned for our outing:

Entrée: Meat à la Meister Brau
Preparation: Submerge steaks in a Meister Brau marinade (2 bottles Meister Brau; ½ bottle garlic salt); set aside in a cool place (such as the Igloo cooler belonging to the lady in site G6 who also let you borrow her OFF!); Duraflame-broil until blackened. Serve with delicious, frosty cans of Meister Brau.

Dessert: Oreo Triple Stuf Cookies
Preparation: Unscrew and re-sandwich Oreo Double Stuf cookie with supplemental toasted marshmallow. Repeat

ad nauseam (literally). Serve with delicious, frosty cans of Meister Brau.

Cigar: To be enjoyed with nightcap of your choice.

V. When to Stop Camping

Camping is best enjoyed in small doses, which is why you must limit your experience to no more than forty-eight hours before driving straight home and going out for Chinese. Though some may disagree (and by "some," I'm referring to my dog, Chloe), take it from me and Richie: the outdoors is a great place to visit but you wouldn't want to live there.

Fear of Fatherhood

C AL IS SITTING on my kitchen floor, licking a sports car. It's one of those cool purple Hot Wheels I used to collect as a kid, but his has more spittle than my whole former fleet. Cal is two. Isn't that an excellent name, Cal? It's Irish or something. He has huge blue eyes and baggy black jeans, and sometimes on Sundays, he'll stop by for a bagel with Linda and Michael. Linda and Michael are brunch friends. They used to be dinner-and-whatever-band-was-playing-the-Paradise friends, but that was before they had Cal. Now when we get together, they spend most of the time replacing the canned goods he enjoys hurling from the cabinets.

A while back, I didn't know how to act around Cal. Frankly, I found his high-maintenance demeanor a little off-putting. But now I hardly pay attention. To Linda and Michael, I mean.

Oh, look! Cal is bouncing his yellow rubber squeaky-ball to Dada! Bouncy-bouncy, that-a-boy!

It seems I'm being plagued by bizarre new thoughts of parenthood. Where once I'd detect a baby and think, "I hope I don't have to sit next to it on the flight," or, "It must get heavy schlepping that thing around on your back all day," lately I find myself thinking, "I wonder what it would be like to be its pappy." I see little Cal with his squeaky-ball, and I imagine playing ball with a kid all my own. I'd buy him a mitt, and we'd work on his pitch. When he was old enough, I'd coach his Little League team, and all the other kids would vote him MVP. "Slugger Zevin," they'd crown him during a victory supper at Chuck E. Cheese's. My face would beam with pride. "Like father, like son," I would remark.

• • •

I *suck* at baseball. The only thing I suck at more than baseball is basketball. Actually, I pretty much suck at all forms of ball. (I do know my way around an eight ball, but you can't take a kid out to play pool. Can you?) The one shining moment in my ball career occurred with the Nerf touch football semifinals at Seashore Day Camp. Miraculously, I intercepted a pass and staved off an asthma attack long enough to charge down the field for a touchdown. I ran the wrong way and won the game for the other team.

Is *that* the kind of father my Slugger deserves? A dad

who can't even play *Nerf*? My son would be a Little League loser, heckled by shouts of "We want a pit-cher, not a belly it-cher!" I guess we could go fishing instead. Are there fish in the Charles River? Maybe I could just take him out for sushi. Wait. I just thought of something. What if Slugger's not a he? What if Slugger's a Sluggette? What sports do girl children do? Gymnastics? What do I know about gymnastics? I can't even touch my toes. Listen to me! I'm a chauvinist pig! I have no business raising a daughter. Little Sluggette would spend her adult life in therapy, discovering that the reason she can't maintain healthy relationships is because her father was a sexist Neanderthal who forced her to do handsprings when she really wanted to take drum lessons.

Drum lessons? How am I supposed to afford drum lessons?

> *Oooooo, lookie lookie how cute little Cal is, smashing his head with his* Arthur Meets the President *book. Woops! There it goes, straight into his mouth. Hey, little fella, if you think that book tastes good, why don't you let Uncle Dan feed you one of these bagels . . .*

When I was Cal's age, my dad read to me every night. *Berenstain Bears; Yertle the Turtle; Kiplinger's Personal Finance* (there were more pictures then). You know what *I* do every night? Whatever I want. I can go out for dinner or get takeout from the Greek place since the only food in our fridge is beer and grape jelly. I can go see a movie that's not rated G. I can blow out of town on a Friday evening without packing an armada of Playskool bathtime boats, or some special off-road stroller that *Consumer Reports* rated the top value under eight thousand dollars. How is it that I can do all these things? Easy. I am a self-absorbed scumbag who thinks only of Me, Me, Me.

So where does that leave Slugger, Slugger, Slugger (or Sluggette)? With some homicidal nanny whenever Daddy feels like whisking Mommy away for an impromptu rendezvous? I can't even afford drum lessons, how am I supposed to afford a nanny? I'd have to work overtime and only see my neglected young offspring when I could drag my sorry ass home at eleven P.M. from my mind-numbing new job at the plant, which I'll have to get because it will put considerably more food on the table than beer and grape jelly— the fruits of the ridiculous "creative" field I have pursued so selfishly and irresponsibly throughout my extended, arrested adolescence.

> *Hey, he's talking! He just said "Brwwww," and then "Vvvvvv." And that last thing he said sounded an awful lot like "Uncle Dan."*

Eventually, I'll advance from absentee father to deadbeat dad. It will happen after Slugger's mom finally gets fed up enough to gather him up in the middle of the night and tear off to the suburbs. Because if you're going to have a kid, you have to live in the suburbs. Because if you don't live in the suburbs, your kid won't go to the right schools. And if your kid doesn't go to the right schools, your kid won't get into the right college.

On second thought, that really shouldn't be a problem

since there's no way I'll ever be able to afford college, anyway, even with my new job at the plant. *Phew.* One less thing to worry about.

> *Shhhh . . . is Cal getting groggy? Look at him there, yawning and rubbing his eyes with his little fingers. Night-night, Weary Willie!*

The idea of being kept awake all night by a screaming, sleepless spawn in soiled Pampers raises a very important question: Does Blue Cross cover vasectomies?

> *Oh, he's fast asleep in his fuzzy triceratops blankey. Innocent; blissful; serene. I am thoroughly mesmerized.*

Disturbing revelation in an ongoing series: I don't want to be a father, I want to be a *baby.*

> *So. Here I am, holding him like Linda and Michael showed me so his head doesn't flop around too much. I gotta say, he's heavier than I thought he'd be. This kid's gonna be a bruiser.*

I wonder where you buy a baseball mitt.

> *This kid's gonna break a lot of hearts.*

I wonder where a kid signs up for drum lessons.

> *This kid's got a load in his Pampers that should be patented by the Department of Defense.*

I wonder who's playing the Paradise tonight.

Confession:

"Going out has been replaced by
 going out for dinner."

Are We Having Food Yet?

I GUESS I KNEW something big had changed when I saw our waiter putting on ManTan in the men's room. I was out for dinner at Temple Bar, a velvety, wall-of-doors-opening-onto-the-sidewalk, would-you-like-fresh-ground-pepper-on-that establishment. I excused myself after ordering the coulées, or the tapenade, or one of those other supersophisticated foodstuffs I find myself trying to pronounce a lot lately. Discovering our waiter touching up his makeup in the men's room was, you know, a little peculiar. Discovering him in this *particular* men's room, however, was truly disturbing.

See, I was no stranger to this particular men's room. Many was the time I relieved myself there when this Temple deal used to be a down-and-dirty (sticky, actually) dive called Nick's Beef and Beer House. My chums and I used to call it "ick's eef and Be Ho," thanks to an aging sign outside that had lost a few letters through the years but was too far gone to give a shit anymore.

Ick's was the kind of place where you'd get beat up if you ever tried ordering coulées. And even after a few too many pitchers of Be, you'd know better than to touch the signature gray gristle masquerading as eef.

Man, I loved that place.

But now that ick's had gentrified into the latest restaurant to serve field greens, not salad, here I was, feeling strangely gentrified myself. I had joined the ranks of former twenty-somethings (I'm talking age *and* take-home pay here) who suddenly find their social lives revolving around places where dinner is served. Or worse, where it's sculpted into multi-tiered figurines so one can never be sure if one's meal was prepared in a kitchen or a kiln.

Let me just pause here to note that I haven't been hanging out at those ultra-spendy, dress-up joints favored by individuals known as "foodies." In fact, finding restaurants that serve reasonably priced figurines is really half the fun. Or at least what passes for fun ever since parties turned into parties of four, and drinking buddies turned into eating buddies.

Once, the kind of dinner I ate four or five nights a week was fortified with eight vitamins and minerals and stayed crispy in milk. Now everyone I know has impassioned beliefs about who serves better shrimp shumai, Jae's or Sweet Chili (answer: Sweet Chili). We know—from experience—that you eat Ethiopian with your hands, and that bi bim bop is not a single by Sha Na Na. We believe the lights could be dimmer, the music lower, the waiter . . . less tan. We have special restaurant matchbook collections.

I, for one, own the goddamn *Zagat* guide.

Can someone please remind me what everyone did for kicks before we became a bunch of restaurant whores? Okay, we went drinking at ick's (man, I loved that place), but what else?

"We just dropped by each other's apartments and hung out," remarked my friend Scott when I raised this question at a "trattoria" forty-five minutes outside of Boston. (Yes, we drove to the suburbs for supper, all right?)

"So how come nobody drops by anymore?" I asked.

"Because now we hate when people drop by," he said, dabbing his bread in the olive oil. "We don't want to hate it, but we do. It interferes with our schedules."

Scott's partner, Sean, chimed in next. Sean is one of the smartest guys I know. Never once have I seen him ask for help with the wine list.

"Here's the thing about restaurants," Sean said. "No cooking, no cleaning, you see your friends, you eat, you pay, you're outta there in an hour and a half. It's, like, a treat."

"Yeah, and you don't have to worry about some bouncer strapping a hospital bracelet to your wrist to show everyone you're over twenty-one," added Megan. "I mean, we're not a bunch of college kids anymore."

To which I replied: "Oh yeah."

• • •

In the beginning, there was brunch. Then that got bourgeois and we began, timidly, to dabble in dinner. We got our feet wet with Indian; tiptoed around Thai. These multi-cultural meals made us feel worldly again, like junior year abroad. But soon, food alone was not enough. We required atmosphere. A guy dressed like a gypsy to serve us tapas! A fusion bistro with a wall-to-wall aquarium! At the very least, a dramatic velvet curtain by the entrance to make us feel we weren't walking into a restaurant but onto a stage.

Oh, the glamour and the glitter.

It was only a matter of time before going out to dinner spawned something even scarier: going out for dessert. It happened most recently when Scott, Sean, me, and the Mrs. drove to the Montreal Jazz Festival. The idea was to take in some actual (by which I mean nonedible) entertainment.

As I listened to the saxophone stylings of Mr. Archie Shepp one evening, I realized I was starved for culture. And when Mr. Shepp finished his set, I realized I was starved for dessert.

What I didn't realize was that LaLoux, the place I planned to eat this dessert (it was in *Zagat's*), would be closing its kitchen five minutes before we arrived. I begged for dessert. I demanded dessert. By God, I was going to get that dessert if I had to slip the maître d' twenty bucks (American).

Voilà! I got dessert. Vanilla ice cream, which I hate. Like the guy said, the kitchen was closed.

Here is the coda to my story: sometimes in life, it takes a bowl of Canadian vanilla ice cream for a guy to realize he's become a pig. And that, my friends, is why I'm trading my days as a restaurant dilettante for a back-to-basics approach.

This week, it's strictly takeout.

Confession:

"I had a little midlife crisis."

Free at Last

A T A CERTAIN stage in life, a certain kind of person dreams of leaving the rat race behind to open a bed-and-breakfast, or taking time off to "do some writing." I am not that kind of person. I have little interest in making my own bed and/or breakfast, much less sharing either with anyone I didn't formally invite. As for taking time off to do some writing, I already did that. At last count, I've clocked in fifteen years.

And therein lay my quandary. At first, I really loved being a freelance writer. I'd get started each day after dinner, bang out some blurbs for a rag I interned at in college, then unwind with a post-work cocktail wherever I knew the bartender. My expenses were $300 a month, half the rent on a one-bedroom I shared with my roommate, Tim. Ours was an egalitarian arrangement: one week I got the bedroom, one week he got the bedroom. Whoever didn't get the bedroom slept on a futon in the living room, which was really pretty comfortable for something we found on the sidewalk.

None of this seemed odd at the time. We were *Simpsons*-watching, backwards-baseball-hat-wearing, *Generation X*–reading twenty-somethings. (Okay, so we never actually finished the book.) The only people who seemed odd were the ones with mortgages, health insurance, special sheds to store their garbage cans.

I am still not sure how it happened, but somewhere down the line I became one of these oddballs. To stave off the collection agents, I had to step up my productivity. I wrote catalogue copy for geriatric bus tours of "Norway, Land of Contrasts." I wrote not one, not two, but three articles about poison ivy. I took a full-time job at *Walking Magazine* (a magazine, by the way, about *walking*), where I'd spend my days in a low-oxygen cubicle, crafting prose about arch supports, or penning reviews of celebrity speed-walking videos. (Actual excerpt: "Sally Struthers sure *struts* her stuff in the hip-flexion segment. . . .")

Actually, I only spent part of my days doing that. I spent the other part sending my more creative (non-bunion-themed) efforts to random agents and publishers, figuring it was prudent to keep those freelance fires burning, and *especially* prudent to do it on company time. It worked. By the time I speed-walked out of my cubicle to revisit the world of self-employment, my career was taking off. I was writing books! Newspaper columns! *Rolling*-friggin'-*Stone,* my friends! It had taken years, but I was doing what I had always dreamed of.

Let me rephrase that. I was always doing what I had dreamed of. Always. Days. Nights. Weekends. During *Simpsons* reruns, for the love of God. My social life disintegrated to an occasional chat with the Person Who Cleans Our Place Every Other Week (please refer to page 105), or a fleeting visit from the UPS guy. Eventually I came down with carpal tunnel syndrome, which required wearing a wrist brace to bed. Strapping on a clip-claw, FYI, is not recommended as a marital aid, and is even less recommended as a sleeping aid. Not that I was doing a whole lot of sleeping. I'd finally turn in around two in the morning, then bolt awake at two-fifteen thinking something like "*Grim!* 'Grim' was the adjective I couldn't think of when I was working on that paragraph all afternoon.

". . . *or was it?*"

Things got really grim the morning I tackled several assignments that were all due the week before. Glancing at my clock, I noted that four hours had passed, and all I had to show for it was the following gem of literary genius: "windshield wiper fluid." "Windshield wiper fluid" was not the title of some forthcoming magnum opus. "Windshield wiper fluid" was a reminder to put more windshield wiper fluid in the car.

● ● ●

Many people are inclined to call this condition "writers' block," but it's really just "grown-ups' block" if you ask me. It's not that you don't know what to write next, it's that you don't know what to *do* next. For some, it means spending years struggling to achieve something, achieving it, then wondering, "Now what?" For others, it means spending years struggling to achieve something, not achieving it, then wondering, "Now what?" My own personal version was this: I'd achieved something in my freelance career I never even wanted to achieve: too much lance, too little free.

It was the "Now what?" part that led to my next quandary.

I decided to do nothing. I don't mean I decided to do nothing about my quandary; I mean I decided to spend my time doing nothing. I had some money socked away, summer was around the corner, and Megan—lucky for both of us—wasn't the type who expected her husband to support her in the style to which she had grown accustomed. (She's always been very good at doing that for herself.)

I called it my hiatus. At first, I felt guilty. This should come as no great surprise since feeling guilty is more of a reflex than an emotion for me. It's like feeling cold, or feeling thirsty. I felt guilty for getting up late, for eating scrambled eggs on a weekday, for reading the whole, entire newspaper—including "School Lunch Wrap-Up"—before heading upstairs to spark up the PowerBook. You may wonder: Why spark up the PowerBook if I was on hiatus? Well, I could say it had something to do with routine, but it had more to do with the aforementioned reflex. What gave *me* the right to shirk my duty as a productive member of society while the rest of the world was pulling their weight? Anyway, I had a lot of work to do. There were new screen-savers to try out, E*Trades to be made, urgent Internet jokes to be forwarded.

Not to mention that working on the computer kept me near my business phone, which had become another appendage for me. Sometimes when it rang, I had to remind myself that I no longer lanced. I wouldn't necessarily remind the client on the other end, though, for fear I'd be dismissed as one more flake who just couldn't cut it. Our conversations would usually sound something like this:

> Client: Zevin! Lou Bingwanger from *Moisty* magazine, where the heck ya been? Listen, I got the perfect article for ya. It's only a millionzillion words long and it's on the history of zippers. When will you be done with it? Tuesday?

> Me: Well, that certainly sounds intriguing, but I am, unfortunately, swamped with more work than I can handle right now. Yes sir, work, work, work, that's all I do. I am all business, all the time.

> Client: Quit workin' so hard! You're gonna go batshit, you hear me?

I'd hang up the phone and resume the day's work, such as switching my computer's Alert Sound from "quack" to "wild eep."

● ● ●

The decision to wean myself from the PowerBook came on the same day, coincidentally enough, that I lost five thousand dollars on a stock tip from one of the many reliable sources to be found in the Yahoo Finance chatroom. Little by little, I'd venture off the premises of my home and into the world outside. Since I really had nowhere to go, I inevitably wound up in a store of some kind. There I'd be, wandering aimlessly about, when I'd find myself in the 99 Cent Shop, loading up on sponges. One day I saw some consignment store I must have passed for years without noticing. I left—in the passenger's seat of the owner's pickup—with a giant wooden bureau for storing all my office supplies. The thing was, my office supplies at the time consisted of a brittle GluStik purloined years before from *Walking Magazine*. One thing led to another, and soon I was on a first-name basis with the shift supervisor at Staples.

And so my hiatus offered its first revelation: it wasn't that I'd been a lousy shopper all these years, it was that my nonstop lancing left no time to exercise my purchasing power. Most of my subsequent purchases turned out to be weather-related for some reason. I mean, yeah, it was just the first week of June, but the fact was, I needed a new snow shovel. The Home Depot guy laughed out loud and told me to come back at Christmas, but I was not roiled. I was in hiatus mode now, and I was a much nicer person. I asked about his family, and promised to spend the coming months thinking seriously about getting a snow blower instead.

This left plenty of time to think seriously about my hiatus itself. I decided to refocus my energy, to put it toward getting more *seasonal* foul-weather merchandise. For example, when I was still lancing, it didn't even occur to me that I needed an umbrella. If I got caught in the rain—which I rarely did, since rain occurs outdoors—what I would do was,

I would get wet. But now that I was on hiatus, an umbrella seemed mandatory. Not just any umbrella—not one of those shitty 99 Cent Shop numbers that flip inside out and leave you looking like those sad sacks who schlep down the street holding a handful of wet metal rods—but an umbrella of *quality*. Ironically, this umbrella was not to be found in any of the numerous department stores I inspected, but in a 1998 SkyMall catalogue, compliments of the Delta Shuttle, that I had thrown in a pile of magazines I figured I'd get to if I ever had the time. And I certainly had the time now. On page 63, I feasted my eyes upon Windbrella®. Windbrella® was roughly one satellite dish in diameter and featured unique patented underside vents, Elastic Shock Cords, and Flexible Memory Rod construction. As if that wasn't enough to sell me right there, Windbrella® also promised to be "lightning resistant." I envisioned myself tap-dancing around town in an electrical storm. I picked up the phone and made my first purchase from an airplane catalogue.

• • •

People generally had one of two responses to the news of my hiatus:

1. The Female Hiatus Response This response tended to be supportive and validating. "A hiatus, how great!" the females would respond, learning I hadn't done a lick of work in three weeks. "Everyone needs time off to recharge! I, too, will go on hiatus!"

2. The Male Hiatus Response Suspicion-laced shock. To hear the male reaction, you'd think I just said I was on "a

shooting spree," or I was on "crystal meth." The men mainly wanted to know how I was supporting myself, assuming, I'm sure, that Megan was taking care of that part, which she wasn't, not because she didn't offer, but because I didn't accept, because if there is one thing that would make me feel *really* guilty, it would be knowing that my wife was bringing home the bacon and I was blowing it on Windbrellas®. So I would tell the guys that, no, Megan's salary wasn't subsidizing me. That after fifteen years of working, I had saved up enough money to take a little time off; that I had reached a kind of psychic plateau in my career and I needed some distance to regain my perspective. I would explain all of this to them in an openhearted and candid manner, and they would look at me empathetically, and finally they would say, "Yeah, I know what you mean. I'd go on hiatus myself if my wife could support me like yours does."

The one question I got from everyone, regardless of gender, was: "So what do you *do* all day?" This was a question with which I was not unfamiliar, having been asked it countless times pre-hiatus by those who had a hard time believing that "writing" was "working." But now it got me thinking. I wasn't doing *nothing* all day. Evidently, I was incapable of doing nothing all day. Evidently, the idea of doing nothing all day really stressed me out. What I was doing all day was keeping busy. Yes, that was it. All day, I was doing busy work.

This seemed rather astounding, since the point of my hiatus was (a) not to be busy, and (b) not to work.

Revelation number two! The reason my hiatus was vaguely dissatisfying was that I'd been depriving myself of fun! So I launched a campaign to have fun. I started mountain biking on these trails near my house. I spent afternoons swimming at Walden Pond. If the weather was inclement, I'd gather up Windbrella® and take in a matinee. And I'll tell you something. Once I began my campaign of fun, that lingering guilt slipped away. In its place came a whole new sensation, a feeling more powerful than any I'd known so far. If I had to describe this feeling, I guess I would call it "crushing alienation." See, when you're sitting around updating your address book or buying foul-weather gear, you never think, "Gee, if only my pals were here to share in the good times." But when you're trying to have *fun,* it doesn't really help that everyone you know is otherwise engaged earning a living and whatnot.

It is times like these when one discovers the true meaning of lunch. Back in my lancing days, I'd meet one of my friends for a sandwich maybe once a week, a quick diversion from whatever deadline loomed upon my return. But now lunch became the apex of my day. I lunched five days a week, scheduled each lunch a week in advance, spent most of my nonlunching hours scouting out potential new persons and places to add to my lunch circuit. Lunchtime became *funtime.* The only glitch was that my dining companions' post-lunch plans consisted of meetings, memos, and conference calls, while my personal to-do list consisted of dessert.

I'd tend to leave these lunches somewhat bloated, and somewhat conflicted. It seemed like *everyone* was killing themselves with work. And I know this sounds odd, but now that I was no longer among them, I held them in higher esteem. There was something honorable about their precisely sixty-minute lunch breaks; something distinguished about the wiry gray hairs they seemed to be sprouting since they took over that project they'd been fighting for all those months. They were grown-ups, and this is what grown-ups did. After lunch, they went back to work.

After lunch, I played with my dog. Chloe is pretty much on permanent hiatus, and though she couldn't ride a mountain bike, she was always available for a game of catch. True, the park was sort of spooky on weekday afternoons—a nanny or two by the seesaw, an old man on a bench feeding Pepperidge Farm croutons to squirrels, me, Chloe—but on one afternoon, I encountered a young woman with a half-dozen dogs of her own. She was wearing a whistle around her neck and a smile on her face. She seemed cheerful, centered. I wondered when she was free for lunch.

It turned out that the dogs weren't hers. She was getting fifteen bucks per hour, per dog. She had twenty-five more to pick up and play with before the day's end. She was a professional dog walker! She had business cards! She was . . . *The Critter Sitter, fully bonded and insured. Member of the Petsitters Society of America.*

I went to work for the Critter Sitter the following week. The way I saw it, here was the most hiatus-friendly activity I'd stumbled upon so far. I'd be having fun out of doors. I'd have constant companionship. And I'd never feel guilty, because not only would I be doing something I loved, I'd be getting paid for it—an impressive fifty cents an hour more than the previous employee, who was forced to resign when his mom said it was interfering with his homework.

The first clients the Critter Sitter contracted out to me were LuLu and Jack, a golden retriever and a beagle, both so freakishly well-behaved that they didn't even attempt to in-spect my crotch upon arrival. I hoped they would be a good influence on Chloe. Each afternoon, I'd swing by their places while their parents were at work, drive them to the park, and let them run around for an hour. Critter Sitter's policy was a sixty-minute excursion, including travel. But since my workload was light, I usually tacked on some over-time to snoop around my clients' households. It seemed that Lulu's parents had recently visited Aruba, judging by a photo album on the coffee table, and as for the new bureau that appeared in Jack's guest bedroom, the one I bought at the consignment place had more room inside.

By July, I was managing a staff of nine dogs, scattered throughout the city and throughout the day. The Critter Sit-ter, pleased with my progress, dropped off keys and written instructions each morning. "Rose, 1pm, catches plastic balls only, not rubber," these notes would read. "Cubby, 4:00, likes one cookie placed on her mat before you leave. Please stay until she eats it." By this point, Critter Sitter had stopped farming out her star dogs, and I was getting the "challenging" ones, as she put it. Dogs like Riley, a foul-breathed mongrel who insisted on sitting up front. On a typical day, I'd have to shuttle over to Riley's condo, drive twenty minutes across town, find a place to park, run up three flights of stairs to get Angel (a/k/a Satan), then spend another fifteen minutes speeding over to Zack's, who, true to Critter Sitter's written instructions, required "gentle coaxing to jump into car." Gentle coaxing, as in "Get in the car *now*, dumbass! Can't you see I'm double-parked in front of a handicapped space?!"

Gone were my pie-in-the-sky dreams of long hikes in the woods. To stay on schedule, "sixty-minute excursions" now meant fifty in the car, ten in whatever empty lot I could find before darting off for my next shift. Without intending to, I'd joined the ranks of the city's kamikaze cab drivers. And not only did I have to pick up my passengers, I also had to pick up after them.

Soon enough, my lunch dates turned into dog-walking dates. "Hey! How about escaping the office and meeting me and the pack for a little break tomorrow!" I'd suggest, convincing each victim that this would be fun. My friend Kevin made the mistake of showing up on a particularly demanding day when I had six dogs at once, including Angel, who had chewed up my Jeep's console while I was busy waiting for Cubby to finish the cookie I'd placed on her goddamn mat. I pulled up to the park ten minutes late, and Kevin was in the middle of his sandwich, the end of which he never got to because it was snatched away by Angel, along with bits of interior auto upholstery.

Just at that moment, all six dogs took off in a blur, some rushing to the far corner to relieve themselves in the sandbox, others terrorizing the toddlers on the seesaw. Angel— always marching to the beat of her own "challenging" drummer—managed to squirm underneath the one barely visible hole in the fence, making her getaway into the surrounding streets.

Kevin sprang into action and chased after Angel while I employed a frantic Sally Struthers sprint through the park to get more plastic bags from my chewed-up console. I had one goal: to swiftly remove the evidence from the sandbox before the playground mommies, who were now screaming at me, could use it against me in a court of law. As a time-saving measure, I hopped the low part of the fence like a hurdler and—*crrrrraaaack!*—proceeded to land on whichever part of one's foot causes one's knee to give out from under him, rendering him splayed out on the sidewalk, immobilized in pain.

Miraculously, Kevin not only captured the fugitive Angel, but also rounded up the rest. I spent the afternoon being X-rayed, limping out of the emergency room on crutches for my torn medial meniscus.

Thus my hiatus came to a close, cut short by a freak dog-walking injury. Instructed to stay off the leg, I could no longer critter-sit, or mountain bike, or shop for stuff I didn't really need. I was forced, under doctor's orders this time, to do nothing. Having spent the past few months learning I wasn't cut out for this Rx, I chose to rest my medial meniscus in a chair placed in front of a PowerBook. And it was there that I began, quite eagerly if you can believe it, composing the very tome you're about to complete.

A burned-out lancer might say my hiatus provided nothing but the promise of arthroscopic surgery. But the truth is, it set me free. Once it was finished, I took time off to do some writing.

About the Author

DAN ZEVIN is the author of *Entry-Level Life* and *The Nearly-wed Handbook*. He has written for *Rolling Stone, Details,* and *Spy* and has been a humor columnist for *Boston Magazine* and *The Boston Phoenix.* A comic correspondent for National Public Radio's WBUR, he also tours campuses nationwide with his satirical seminars on post-college coping. He lives with his wife, Megan Tingley, and their mutt, Chloe Tingley-Zevin, in Cambridge, Massachusetts, where he takes great pride in his lawn. For more information, visit www.danzevin.com.